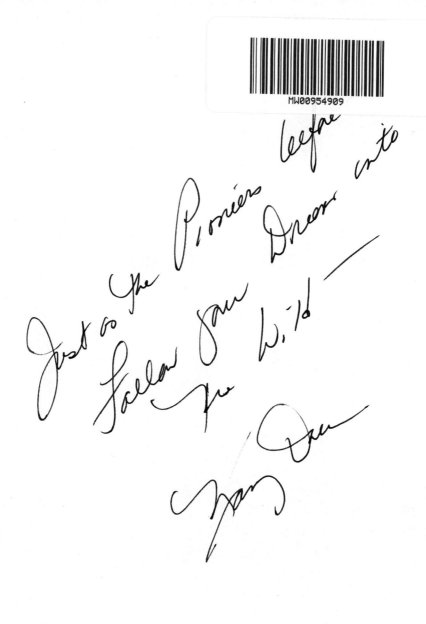

Just as the Pioneers before
Fallow your Dreams into
the Wild

WILD FLORIDA THE WAY IT WAS

AS TOLD BY THE PIONEER "COW HUNTERS" AND "HUNTRESSES" WHO LIVED IT

ALSO BY NANCY DALE

Where the Swallowtail Kite Soars: The Legacies of Glades County, Florida and the Vanishing Wilderness
ISBN: 0-595-32557-2

Would Do, Could Do, and Made Do: The Florida Pioneer "Cow Hunters" Who Tamed the Last Frontier
ISBN: 0-595-41568-7

"The Tattered Flag"
The Treasure Coast Writers Guild: An Anthology of Selected Stories
ISBN: 1-59872-075-9

WILD FLORIDA THE WAY IT WAS

AS TOLD BY THE PIONEER "COW HUNTERS" AND "HUNTRESSES" WHO LIVED IT

iUniverse books may be ordered through booksellers or by contacting:

iUniverse
1663 Liberty Drive
Bloomington, IN 47403
www.iuniverse.com
1-800-Authors (1-800-288-4677)

Because of the dynamic nature of the Internet, any Web addresses or links contained in this book may have changed since publication and may no longer be valid. The views expressed in this work are solely those of the author and do not necessarily reflect the views of the publisher, and the publisher hereby disclaims any responsibility for them.

ISBN: 978-0-595-51104-4 (pbk)
ISBN: 978-0-595-51747-3 (cloth)
ISBN: 978-0-595-61766-1 (ebk)

Printed in the United States of America

iUniverse Rev. 12/9/08

Wild Florida The Way It Was

AS TOLD BY THE PIONEER "COW HUNTERS" AND "HUNTRESSES" WHO LIVED IT

NANCY DALE

iUniverse, Inc.
New York   Bloomington

Lone Cypress
Fisheating Creek

CREDITS

EDITOR:
ANNALANE HARRIS

TECHNOLOGY DESIGN LAYOUT:
HEATH DANIELS

COVER PHOTO:
"IRIS WALL"
INDIANTOWN, FLORIDA
BY CAROLYN LAWRENCE

PHOTO OF NANCY DALE
BY DAVE TRAPHAGEN

Caloosahatchee River
Moore Haven

TO MY GRANDCHILDEN
ALEXA AND MAXX

May you grow-up with an appreciation
for the Land and Native Florida

"Human subtlety will never devise an invention
more beautiful, simpler, or more direct than does
Nature, because in her inventions nothing is lacking
and nothing is superfluous."

Leonardo da Vinci

Photo by Samantha Davis

This day will never return…..

Live each day as the last… and best.

Nancy Dale

CONTENTS

PART II
KEEPING THE LEGEND ALIVE: FLORIDA CRACKER HERITAGE

EPILOGUE OLD FLORIDA IN THE 21ST CENTURY

WITH APPRECIATION

Writing is a solidarity path and a collaborative effort woven together by intrinsic values. To everyone who took the time to tell me their personal stories, your inspiring lives will always linger in my thoughts and spirit.

Without the support, constructive reviews, suggestions, and talent of others, this project would have stalled with many blank pages and unfinished thoughts. But as way leads onto way, obstacles eventually disappear, fortitude rises to persistence, and a joint quest comes to an end with a time for contemplation.

Thanks to all who paused along the way to offer creativity and expertise. Thank you to Jim Handley and the Florida Cattleman's Association for their continued support and Charlie Stevens. To my sister and Editor, Annalane Harris, teacher at Fairlawn Elementary school (Miami), thanks for the many times you went out of your way to provide a respite and common sense. To Heath Daniels, Administrative Specialist, Edison College (LaBelle), thank you for your forever persistence and cheer in sorting through this publishing maze. To Jerel Eller, Manager, Office Max (Sebring), thanks for assisting me in meeting frantic deadlines with quality production. To my long time friends, Pattie Parker and "John Who Watches the Grass Grow," thank you!

Through the many unexpected perils of shaping a book into its final living worthiness, there evolves a perspective: "If you want to see the rainbow, you have to really love the rain."

PREFACE

A Living Heritage

Traveling into the past is an adventure. As a Scribner of those who lived through the days when life was created with grit, wit, and fortitude, it was a privilege.

Walking beside these men and women, listening to them tell their true stories about wild Florida, the way it was, and how they lived it, is an historic legend.

If they had a dream, they followed it; if they stumbled along the way, it was only in passing as they packed up their gear, tightened their boot straps and started a new day. The values expressed in their stories, reflected in their lives are admirable, but in their quiet way they don't want to be penned as "heroes or heroines," it was just what they had to do to survive.

Along the way, they kept their wit with a twinkle of the eye weaving long tales by the campfire glittering like fireflies into the falling night. This is how they remembered those hard times.

From those who passed this way before, handing down their code of ethics and dedication to the land is the living heritage that these pioneers graciously offer to future generations as lessons, not to be forgotten, but hopefully, lived.

As a continuing epic, this book is a tribute to the living heritage of the Florida "Cow Hunters" and "Huntresses" past and present.

FORWARD

BY

DUCK SMITH

Ken McLeod (Wauchula), Norman Proveaux (Myaaka) and Duck Smith (Bar Crescent S Ranch, Wauchula)

Those of us here in Florida, who have an interest in and a love for history that relates to the cattle industry and ranching in Florida during the early 1900's are blessed indeed to have someone such as Nancy Dale, take the time and show the interest to research and study the lives of some of the folks who lived and survived ranching as a way of life here in Florida almost 100 years ago.

The characters and stories Nancy has chosen to include in her new writings will both entertain you and touch your heart. These folks had to exhibit a lot of courage, as well as a lot of just plain "want to," to be able to make a go of it and live to tell of their experiences.

Those of us who love the land and the way of life, ranching can "provide" for us and our families, including our grandchildren. We owe a debt of gratitude to Nancy Dale for her work and effort. Let us just hope that 100 years from now, should the Lord tarry that long, there will still be some ranching in Florida to write about, as we try to adjust and survive the changes the cowman faces here in Florida.

Thank you again, Nancy, for your commitment to our history.

God Bless,

Duck Smith – Rancher

Hardee County

INTRODUCTION

Florida's Birth From The Bottom Of The Sea

Two and a half million years ago massive ocean currents swept equatorial heat to the Northern Hemisphere of the Earth and mile-deep glaciers formed over much of the North American continent. Fresh water that otherwise would have flowed to the sea was sucked up in icy masses raising from the depths of the ocean the limestone mass of the Florida peninsula. Sea levels along the crusted shoreline fluctuated many times over geological history as the mysterious creatures of the deep ruled the seas. The oceans were owned by giant sharks, whales and mammals while giant sloths, mammoths, bison and herds of saber tooth tigers roamed the continent. During the interglacial period, 2 to 1.7 million years ago, the Caloosahatchee Formation in Central Florida, guarded the fossils of its last habitation in a submerged record of their existence.

As the glaciers retreated, a stark, vast Florida peninsula laid waste, not wet with swamps or an abundance of water as it became thousands of years later, but with a drier xerix of low lying vegetation.

It was not until the last Pleistocene period, twelve thousand years ago, that the first humans foraged their way into North America venturing across the dry land bridge between Siberia and Alaska. They lived in a Florida twice the size that it is today exposing vast expanses of the present continental shelf. Coasts were inland, even upland, with Gulf of Mexico shorelines 50 miles westward than present day submerged beneath fathoms of ocean water. Florida's dramatic climatic history altered the borders of the coast with Hendry County, west of Lake Okeechobee, at one time taunting a crystal beach when waters were flooding the inland plants. The

Moores Creek
Photo by Samantha Davis

maximum extent of the glacial period was about 18,000 years ago, with the ice melting very fast some 11,000 years ago. The sea level was higher in Florida by 20 to 30 feet when a shallow tropical sea covered the southern half o f the peninsula. The ecology of the new land mass was a mosaic of vegetation, punctuated with forest and savannas.

The Paleo-Indians where tribal hunters that competed with territorial game in their search for food. The ingenuity of the early Paleo-Indian as hunters began their struggle for survival by quarrying projective tools, sharpening and shaping lancelet missiles to take down huge prey, that sank their massive bodies into the cool artisan waters, unconscious of the skilled hunters along the river's edge poised to sink their spears into their flesh. Some paleontologists contribute the extinction of the thick heavily built mastodon, longer than the other two specifies of mammoths present in Florida.

Lodged in rivers and springs across Central Florida, fossils of the extinct beast have been unearthed in Wakulla Springs and on the Aucilla River where, also, a 13 thousand-year-old giant tortoise, impaled by a wooden spear, was found in Little Salt Spring, Sarasota County.

There were other beasts of prey that the Paleo-Indians challenged such as the giant armadillo with thirty-six teeth and hundreds upon hundreds of sharp scutes, bison, deer and tapirs, a semi-aquatic animal with a long, flexible nose like an elephant's trunk. There was the giant 500 pound, eight foot beaver with upper incisors that were more than ten inches in lengths. Gentler beasts also inhabited the peninsula with camels living in abundance on the grasslands and a canopy of more than 267 species of birds gracing the sky whose fragile remains today are still difficult to classify.

During the Archaic (ancient) period, the Paleo-Indians improved their technology as shorelines moved inland and the sea became a prime source of plentiful food. They carved, from a flint like stone called chert, a variety of small tools for fishing, gathering plants, and hunting the evolved smaller mammals and reptiles.

The advance and retreat of glaciers through the Great Lakes region (near as far south as Florida) is believed by paleontologists to have fluctuated during the Paleo-Indian Period of the late Pleistocene period approximately 12 to 20 thousand years ago and lasted some 3,000 years.

For the last 6 to 8 thousand years, the ecosystem and environmental conditions in Southern Florida have remained basically stable providing conditions for aboriginal camps to survive.

Fisheating Creek
Palmdale

Archeological researchers estimate that it was during the pre-ceramic period from 6500 to 2000 BC, that early Indians lived across southwest Florida, evidenced by fish hooks, harpoon points and dugout canoes discovered in Lee County. By 1000 BC, an aboriginal population settled at Ft. Center on Fisheating Creek near Lakeport and findings from the site suggest the group was one of the first to practice agriculture in Florida. These early people are said to have cultivated maize (corn) that could be stored to establish, and seasonally equalize, their food supply. They had a technique for altering the Savannah topography, making circle ditches that provided drained fields for planting. The ditch spoil was possibly a source of fertilizing mulch. Pollen analysis indicates that squash and beans may also have been cultivated.

Fort Center was occupied for more than 2,000 years by the stable Belle Glade Indian culture that regenerated the site over the generations with fossils recovered from the Pleistocene Epoch. It is believed that these fossils were washed up on the higher ground and may have been used by Native cultures with a distance in time of more than a million years apart.

From 500 A.D., other historic Indian mound villages have been discovered in Florida, including the preserved site in Ortona that was a complex society of ancient Indians. The early traders at Ortona used the waterway that then networked Charlotte Harbor up the Caloosahatcchee through some of the longest canals in North American crossing wet prairies and waterfalls that linked to larger channels. One of these series of canals connected Pine Island to the Caloosahatchee, with what is now Cape Coral, to Lake Okeechobee; thus, these people were the first humans to carve a river network between the Caloosahatchee and Lake Okeechobee in Central Florida. The early river travelers and agriculturists of Ortona are believed to have migrated from South America and brought with them an adaptation to agricultural practices.

Yet, over twelve millennia and twelve thousand years, there is still much of Florida's human history buried silently beneath our feet. The early Indian tribes whose lifestyle and culture is recorded in their artifacts include the Caloosa warriors, the Ocale, and Apalachee. Their legacy, as a people, reflects their ingenuity to tame the wilderness and enrich their lives from resources provided by Nature.

Easter Sunday, March 27, 1513, the "Holy Day of Flowers," Spanish explorer Ponce de Leon riding the high seas of the Atlantic Ocean, spied through his tiny eyeglass sparks of sunlight on glassy waves sliding along the shoreline of a beach. He scanned the far horizon, his thirsty eyes drinking in the welcomed sight of what he hoped to be the promised land of gold and fountain of youth.

When Ponce de Leon arrived, there were already approximately 350,000 Indians inhabiting the peninsula, but many of the indigenous Indians were gradually wiped out by disease, pestilence and slavery introduced by European settlers.

Florida's destiny was created by cataclysmic natural change. When man arrived with a "universal process of knowing," termed by Plato as *anima mundi,* or "world soul" the dimensions of "reality" were redefined. Today, Florida is the product of Nature's "design" and man-made consciousness. However, in the end, the small dimple of man's influence is yet to be determined.

DESIGN

I found a dimpled spider, fat and white,
On a white heal-all, holding up a moth
Like a white piece of rigid satin cloth--
Assorted characters of death and blight
Mixed ready to begin the morning right,
Like the ingredients of a witches' broth--
A snow-drop spider, a flower like a froth,
And dead wings carried like a paper kite.

What had that flower to do with being white,
The wayside blue and innocent heal-all?
What brought the kindred spider to that height,
Then steered the white moth thither in the night?
What but design of darkness to appall?--
If design govern in a thing so small.

ROBERT FROST

PART I

ONE

"THERE ARE NO SET ANSWERS IN LIFE, BUT DO SOMETHING AS IT BEATS FAILURE, AND KEEP TRYING,"

ELWYN AND ELDA MAE BASS OF BASINGER

Approaching the winding, graceful curve of the Kissimmee River cutting through miles of pasture along U.S. 98 in Okeechobee County, travelers are welcomed into "Bassinger" by a small green roadside sign. Then crossing over the meandering Kissimmee into Highlands County towards Sebring, an engraved marker on the Edna Pearce Lockett estate commemorates Fort "Basinger," one of sixty-four Civil War outposts Zachary Taylor plotted and

1

built in twenty mile grids across Florida during the bounty hunting days of the 1800s Seminole Indian Wars.

But there has been an ongoing mystery over the years about the spelling of the community of "Basinger" in Okeechobee County and "Fort Bassinger" in Highlands County across the River. Is the "Basinger "community spelled with one "s" and "Fort Bassinger" across the River spelled with two? The sign markers don't even agree. This long-standing mystery, however, is clarified by pioneer "cow hunter" Elwyn Bass, who has been a rancher for more than forty years in the "Basinger" community. "There are two 'Basingers,' Fort "Bassinger" on the east side of the river in Highlands County is spelled with two 'ss' and our community across the river is spelled with one 's,' but over the years the spelling has changed two or three times." The old official Florida Fort records, according to research historian Don Cox, notes that "Fort Basinger is spelled with one "s," in conflict with a December 8, 1897 article in the *Kissimmee Valley Gazette* written by early Basinger settler and Notary Public, Robert LaMartin. He writes that Union Army Colonel Zachary Taylor moved more than a thousand troops along the Kissimmee River from Tampa during the Second Seminole Indian War with orders to destroy or capture Indians. Bounty hunters were paid $500 for warriors, $250 for women, and $100 for children. LaMartin writes that Colonel Taylor erected a stockade and named it Fort "Bassinger" after Lt. William E. "Bassinger" who was killed in the Dade Massacre of 1835.

"It wasn't until after the Indian Wars that pioneers north of Kissimmee began to settle around Fort Mead, Basinger, and Okeechobee. Most cattle people moved to the area for better grass and a better life," says Elwyn, as Basinger was one of the first "cow towns" around Lake Okeechobee. Arriving in the 1800s, the first settlers were the Parkers, Holmes, Raulersons, Chandlers, Underhills and others. After the Civil War, and by the turn of the Century, Basinger became a bustling community of ranchers, farmers, and trappers taunting two hotels, a general store, and post office.

From 1894-1920, Basinger's economy grew not only from the developing cattle industry but from the steamboat business along the Kissimmee. Riverboats plied the waters from Kissimmee to Basinger hauling supplies for ranchers including freight, alligator hides, otter and coon skins, oranges, grapefruit and passengers with their horses. But, Basinger's steamboat industry gradually died out when highways were constructed and the railroad by-passed the community for a depot in Okeechobee.

However, as reporter Robert LaMartin reported in the 1897 issue of the *Kissimmee Valley Gazette,* the cattle business thrived in Basinger:

We are having delightful weather at present with pleasant showers of rain. Another bunch of beef cattle passed through to Tampa for shipment to Cuba gathered by E. O. Morgan and H. H. Holmes, and others who sold a bunch of 195 head of mixed beef to Z. King of Fort Ogden. Al Alderman drove a bunch of 100 head of extra fat beef cattle sold to E.O. Morgan and consigned to Alderman and Raulerson. Bassinger tenders her compliments to the journalistic union of the Valley and Gazette. May its voyage of life be large and prosperous. May it be rich in the field of moral, literary, and political thought, and its shadow never grow less.

"My granddaddy, James and Christine Durrance bought this track of land in

1903 when he was still riding the cattle trails," says Elywn who now lives at the original homestead "but it wasn't until 1945 after World War II that President Roosevelt started to put more money into roads and utilities in Florida, as we were behind in new things and didn't even have electricity."

Elwyn's daddy, Oscar Bass, was born in 1898 and grew up around Bull Creek near Kenansville. It was in 1929, after the family re-settled in Basinger that Oscar Bass met and married Zona Durance at the little Basinger Church of the Brethren after a Wednesday night prayer meeting. "The church still exists, but the name has been changed to the Basinger Christian Brethren Church," says

Elda Mae, the youngest of the Bass' four children. The other siblings include J.C., the oldest, Elwyn, next, then Glenn and Elda Mae.

Zona and Oscar resided in Okeechobee where he owned a barber shop until the booming 1900s community went bust in the Great Depression. The day after Zona and Oscar were married, he went to the bank and it was closed. "Mama and daddy had only $8.50 to pay the rent, buy some furniture, and

to live on," says Elda Mae, recalling the stories her daddy told her about their survival during those difficult times. "He would work at anything to make money but with two dollars you could buy all kinds of things," adds Elwyn. "Daddy tried to keep the barbershop open but no one was getting haircuts. He worked there during the day and grew out hogs at the ranch on days off until the 40's. In those days, there were no fence laws and you could make a 'hog claim' on hogs running loose as they were domestic breeds and not considered 'wild.' Also, around the St. John's River, you could make 'wild horse claims' but there wasn't much money in horses." However, the family survived and the ranch grew.

As more Southerners migrated into Florida in the 1800-1900s, they continued the tradition of passing on family names to their children. Elwyn Bass, 75, said his mama named him after a cousin. "I never saw anyone with my name until I was in my twenties."

Although Elda Mae, the lone female sibling in the family, says she "always wanted to be a cowgirl and begged to go everywhere with my brothers, but I was a girl. All three of my brothers looked after me and were protective but I mostly stayed home as there was no money to travel. But, before I started school, Daddy taught me how to put marks on a  paper to count cattle." Elda Mae says she was also called a "tar baby" during the screwworm epidemic as "I used a mop or sometimes used my hand to put tar on a calf's ears and naval or any open cuts. I always tagged along as a helper."

"When daddy had jobs working cattle for others, he camped out or stayed at someone's house. The boys fed the animals and went to school. Daddy had only one working horse, so in the first grade Elwyn and J.C. walked 3 ½ half miles to school. In 1946, we lived at Eagle Bay when the big hurricane hit. The Basinger bridge was taken out and we needed to feed some cattle, so we camped at the ranch. The boys went to school in Okeechobee, so the Basinger kids had to row across the slough to the other side to catch the bus. But Mama made us go to school even when we tried to 'pretend sick;' she knew all the excuses and would say that we would feel better if we went to school."

"Daddy was also protective of the boys. Although he 'cowboyed' and broke horses, he said there wasn't much money in it, just about $50.00 a horse. Daddy talked away from riding bulls and rodeoing as there were some kin folks with broken legs and teeth knocked out," says Elda Mae. "Daddy said if you were going to be a rodeo rider," Elwyn emphasizes, "you needed to learn how to do it right, not to get hurt." The Bass' cousin's grandson, Chase Bass, has learned to "do it right" and recently became the Okeechobee High School horseback and bronco-riding champ. Although Elwyn didn't ride the rodeo circuit, he had his share of excitement in cattle round-ups that are today re-enacted in the arena to thrill fans.

In one unforeseen event, Elwyn was rounding up cows at Trout Creek when he got caught in a wild stampede. "I had a bunch of cows together when they started to run. Cattle will run until they kill themselves against trees or give out. If one gets scared, they all run and real fast. We had to wait until first light to circle the herd with our cur dogs so we could see gopher holes." According to Elwyn, "cur dogs are bred to perform specific duties as part of the cow crew. They are bred to 'catch' the cattle, soon learning to keep up, not to get killed. For some dogs, it is natural to be in front and stop the cows as the horses gallop up. Some 'heel dogs' nip at the back driving the cows. But the first thing a dog has to learn is 'to mind;' they are not pets." Elwyn laughed saying, "my wife, Pat, has ruined some dogs right now, making them pets." Elwyn has three children, Marilyn, Quinn, and Brian by his first wife, Irma. He married Pat Rose in 1990; she has two children and five grandchildren.

Growing up in wild Florida meant, in the words of Oscar Bass, "taking it as it comes." One day thirteen year old Elwyn was parting steers with his grandpa at Dad's Island driving them to Ft. Drum, "when one of the steers slipped out and I had to catch her. I galloped around to see how good I had done when a steer pulled up against my horse and tried to hook it. My saddle went off and across the steer's back as the horse started running and I still had hold of the reins. I felt so scared I didn't turn to see if anyone was watching. But shaking his head, Grandpa said, 'Sonny boy, you better get back on your horse before that steer gets you!' Brahman cows will confront you; they are mean as bulls."

As a way of life, Elwyn and Elda Mae's daddy followed cattle to earn a living. In the 1930-40s, he worked for Lykes Brothers in Palmdale making $40 a month then for awhile lived in Arcadia. As a teen, Elwyn "grew up everywhere." In the 40's he helped load cattle on trains going to Kentucky and Texas. He sold steers for slaughter when only a few calves were sold as "there wasn't a market in those days for calves. Daddy tried to raise one bunch of steers on grass for sale to the slaughter people when they would come by. The steers weighed about 1,100 pounds and brought 10 cents a pound; calves sold at 16 cents a pound."

Elwyn also worked on and off for Buck Mann and Maxcy in the late 50's. "We had to gather Mann and Maxcy's cattle that got mixed up then we parted them out. There were about 10,000 head of cattle. We swam the cattle on the river then put about 1,000 cows into a small pasture called a 'crevasse' to corner them up. We sorted them out by earmarks and brands using dogs. Elwyn tells a story about pioneer rancher Buck Mann's daddy in the 1940s, although he says "it's hearsay. Mann sold 1,000 head of cattle for $5.00 a head; that's not much. Today, a 400-600 pound calf sells for about $1.00 a pound. In the 50's, a 200 pound calf sold for $50."

Since 'cow hunters' were nomadic, they lived mostly in isolation, camping out with their cattle on long drives across Florida. When they settled down at home, they had a different view of life. Punctuated with a few laughs, Elwyn recalls his grandpa's words: "When you can see a neighbor's smoke, it's time to move. It took three moves to equal one 'burn out.' When the old timers traveled to Florida in wagons or downstream in boats, you had to leave a lot of stuff behind, that was a 'burn out.'" But, this was also the "cow hunter" way.

Throughout the history of the cattle industry and today, ranchers have had to deal with rounds of potentially threatening diseases and epidemics. Elwyn was born during the outbreak of the first fever ticks when there was "no insecticide, no medicine, only the arsenic dipping vats. Daddy and his brothers were hired by the government as 'range riders' to ride behind cattle owners and shoot any wildlife that might carry the ticks. The ticks were not just on warm-blooded animals but also on gopher turtles and snakes. Today, there are still diseases with more confinement and importation of cattle from foreign countries."

Although Elda Mae says the Bass children were sheltered, they were able to deal with whatever confronted them and made choices for the better. "Parents didn't know how to raise children then, but they did it. We were never out of food, we all got what we needed. They always did the best they could and we were all loved." In a few pointed words, Elwyn expresses the philosophy he lives by today learned from his parents and through his own experience: "There are no set answers in life but do something, as it beats failure, and keep trying. You don't get rich in the cattle business but you can make a living,"

Elda Mae and Elwyn agree that the future of Florida agriculture depends on teaching youths about the industry. "This could be the last generation for the land if kids in school don't have an understanding of it. Some young people have a blank look when you talk about making a living off the land," said Elda

Mae. "If we don't feed our nation, we are in trouble. We need to bridge the gap. Many young people don't object to the government; they don't seem to realize the control the government has on water regulations, how much water is used, even if you dig a hole or put in a reservoir, and the threat of eminent domain taking private property."

"In Florida, the government is unfriendly to agriculture. Today, when a young kid graduates from high school or college, unless his family has property, it's hard to start a cattle ranch. To go into the cattle business today, you have to work everyday in town on a second job to stay in business. It takes so many years to make a living. It is very sad," Elda Mae laments.

"The cattle industry has changed the most over the last ten years. We've been here thirty or forty years. Today, there are more regulations, and it's hard to get ahead with the expensive price of land. The population growth in Florida is against agriculture. People like domestic agricultural products but they don't realize what it takes to maintain it; Nature has a fragile balance."

"At one time around here, we had a co-op slaughterhouse, but it cost millions of dollars for inspections, union workers, and management. It was hard to find business people to get into beef," Elda Mae stresses. "There also were a number of slaughterhouses in Florida, one at Center Hill (north of Brooksville), Haines City, and Tampa. In the days of free, open range and slaughterhouses, ranchers provided the main source of beef for America." "Today, prices are good for cow-calf operations," ads Elwyn, "and I am hopeful about the future.

I believe that the cattle industry will always be around in Florida as long as there is a worldwide demand for beef."

Today, the Bass' run a family business with Elwyn and Pat maintaining a small registered herd of both cracker horses and cows. They sell some cracker calves but "there is not much future in the cracker horse business. The Florida cracker cows," Elwyn explains, "are a close kin to the Mexican 'bull fighting' cows or 'Corrientes' and have a distinct personality. Florida 'cracker cows' are also small and need more space because they have horns. They are inquisitive, alert, not like the English type cow that is more 'sleepy.' The rations also make the difference as the cracker cow can survive drought when there is no grass."

The Spanish Conquistadors brought the "Corriente" horned steer into the Americas in the 9th Century when they drove the Moors out of the Iberian Peninsula and brought cattle to the plains of Andalusia. By the 13th Century, Andalusian settlers in 1493 brought their early ranching practices to Hispaniola and the New World. Under the Spanish crown's mission to colonize the Americas on Christopher Columbus' second voyage in 1493, he brought cargos of cattle to the Canary Islands. In order to survive the long voyage, it is speculated that cattle were suspended in slings to protect them from injury as the ship rolled over the high seas. By 1565, cattle and Spanish conquest were linked to settlements in Puerto Rico, Panama, Cuba, México, South America, Jamaica and Florida.

The descendants of the Spanish cattle developed under centuries of natural selection in the high desert of Mexico's central plateau and can still be found on isolated plateaus. These cattle are small, agile, hardy, and have a good disposition. Florida "scrub cattle" are the descendants of those animals that were running wild on the peninsula left by the Spanish Conquistadors that were captured and bred by pioneer "cow hunters." This was the birth of the Florida cattle industry.

Today, the Florida cattle industry is a major economic engine in agriculture but is "in jeopardy" as Elwyn puts it: "In the early days, the horse was used to pull the cart; now the cart pulls the horse." But cattle ranching still thrives in Basinger and is the heartbeat of this unincorporated area of Okeechobee County.

Basinger is located on the shoulder of the second largest freshwater lake in the United States, Lake Okeechobee that was formed six thousand years ago when the shallow sea that once covered South and Central Florida, receded.

Okeechobee County was named after the Lake from the Hitchiti words "oka" (water) and "chobi" (big). It was also previously called Macaco and Mayaimi, the later term the origin of the City of Miami.

According to the 2000 Census, the population of Okeechobee County was 35,910; there are 483 registered voters in Basinger.

TWO

"RIDIN' BULLS AND ROPIN' STEERS"
PIONEER "COW HUNTER" AVON PARK

GENE CARTER

At eighteen years old, Florida born Gene Carter struck out on his own to follow his star to the great Northwest joining the Harley Roth Rodeo in Rapid City, North Dakota. It was Gene Carter's ambition to one day become a championship bull and bronc rider, a goal he achieved many bucking bulls and wild horses later. For five years from 1955-58, he earned the title as one of Florida's greatest "Best All Round Bull Riders and Bronc Riders." In his unassuming manner, 6'1" Gene Carter of Avon Park said, "If you didn't like it, you didn't do it."

Not all ranchers translate their everyday roping and riding skills into the rodeo arena but when Harley Roth came to buy some bulldogging steers from his daddy, Gene Carter connected with his future. Although Gene Carter did not compete in the event, he describes the challenge of man and animal against the clock. "In the rodeo, one rider, a 'hazer' punches the steer over to the bulldogger on the left who jumps off the horse and throws the 650-700 pound calf. You put a 'Nelson' on its head and horn as you twist it over until all four feet are out straight. The clock begins when you leave the shoot." Today's record in bulldogging is 3-3/10 second. The record time in the 1950s was 16 seconds.

It wasn't enough to be a tough bronc rider, Gene Carter also aspired to take on bucking bulls. "It's between you and the animal. You cannot predict the bull, there is no way to judge them. Bulls don't always turn the same direction; it depends on the nature of the bull. Sometimes they will go one way and then sometimes another; sometimes he will try to hook you, and sometimes he just wants to get out of the way." Fifty percent of bull riders are right handed; Gene rides with the left.

As far as specific techniques to stay on the bull, Gene says, "There's nothing special to know but there are some techniques. You better learn to keep your balance and adapt to the bull. When the bull jumps high you have to jump higher, not learn back but forward, keep your feet down, and hand in the air.

You use the spurs and knees to hold on, however, if you spur the bull during the eight seconds, you get higher points."

In the winter, Gene Carter followed the rodeo circuit to Kissimmee, Florida and the Silver Spurs Rodeo that began in the 1940s. "It was easier here as the bulls were not as big or strong. There was more grass in the Dakotas and they were fed on grain."

"The bucking bulls today are a genetic cross-breed with Brahman bulls and Angus cows to get a Brangus bull. The life of a rodeo bull is about eight years before they get worn out. For a bulldogger, a career can extend to about 30 years old if one can survive with livable injuries and still ride. I rodeod for about ten years." Gene Carter did not sustain any serious injuries until he broke his shoulder in 1960 and needed to have a pin inserted; then he "called it quits." He was 28 years old.

During his return to Florida, Gene and his first wife decided to live in Avon Park. "When I finished the rodeo career, I returned to the only job I knew, to be a 'cowboy'." Most people in Florida had family owned cow herds. By now the couple had five children (one is now deceased). It was not until twenty years later after his first marriage ended, that Gene ran into Margie Carter, who he had not "talked to but once and never talked to her again over all those years." Margie, a widow, lived in Avon Park with her three children.

Margie and her parents moved there when she was eight. Unlike Gene's background from a "cow hunter" family, Margie's father was a lawyer. When Gene met Margie again it was when he worked at the Gene Fulford, KICCO Ranch on Highway 60. Margie's son also worked there and one day she came to see him. "I saw her crossing the yard and said to myself, 'Dad gum, there's Margie.' I walked over and talked to her. It went well." One year later, in 1978, they were married at the courthouse in Wauchula and had an instant family of seven children.

Due to the nature of the cattle business, Gene move around to various ranches, working in Immokalee for Consolidated Immokalee Cattle "owned by a business man in New York City that didn't know a horse from a cow. In the 60-70s, we gathered up calves in pens and hauled them by truck to the Okeechobee Livestock Market."

"Immokalee is good for cattle. Farmers cleared the land for vegetables that cultured it; Immokalee has wide prairies, marshes, and palmettos. To get the cows out of the muck and swamp, we roped them and used about seven dogs to catch them. After Immokalee, I bought my own herd. In the 40s when fence laws were passed, you bought all the land you could to support your cows. You need about twenty-five acres per cow, which cost then from $3,000 to $10,000. You could keep steers and grow them out but steers get bigger and compete with cows. However, land in Florida is good and there was a lot of it in those days. Then, the government passed fence laws because they didn't want any wrecks on the new roads. It was the population increase and cars that closed the open range."

Today, Gene and Margie are cattle ranches on the rolling hills of Avon Park surrounded by the aroma of orange groves and native habitat. They have horses, Brahman crossbred cows, and three emus. In the wooden stable behind the house is where Gene's trusty workhorse Dexter is penned. Gene raised Dexter from a colt and when Gene is saddled on him, he responds with the slightest cue from the reins. Running beside the two is Gene's cur dog, Spot, that is as respective to Gene as he is to granddaughter, 7 month old Rylee Kay Culbertson. Margie always played a major role as a "cow girl." Although she didn't rope or ride as part of the cow crew she kept them nurtured with her good food and brought home cooked meals out to the cow camps wherever they were. "By the 60-70s, the younger generation built screened in structures with bunk beds and wouldn't sleep out on the ground," added Gene Carter.

Many of the Carter family members work on the ranch. Since Gene has been a cowboy all his life, he is passing on the ranching tradition to his children and grandchildren, who are both cowboys and cowgirls on his crew. The Carters' lease 16,000 acres on the 109,000-acre Avon Park Air Force Bombing Range (APAFBR) that was acquired by the government in 1942 to train military pilots and the army in ground-to-air war strategies.

Between 1942 and 1997, the United States government acquired 218,883.88 acres for the Avon Park Bombing Range straddling Highlands-Polk counties. During World War II, it was called Avon Park Army Air Field and was used as a training base for B-17 aircraft for air-to-ground bombing activity.

According to a 10 April 1942 newspaper article, Avon Park Air Force used the range to detonate bombs ranging in size from 15-pound practice bombs to 2000-pound demolition bombs containing 2 tons of high explosives. In July 1946, the Avon Park Army Air Field had 26 thousand M1A1 practice bombs stored in an open area. In 1947, the base was deactivated and placed in caretaker status. In 1949, the base was transferred to the Air Force and in 1958, became the Avon Park Air Force Bombing Range when a small city was built that included residence and mess halls, barracks, a chapel, dorms, fire station, and administration buildings. In 2006, the Navy increased the number of annual bombings runs on the range from 6,900 to 9,998 when the Vieques, Puerto Rico target operations were phased out.

The mission of the APAFBR is to manage special use airspace, assets, and diversified training programs for military ground troops. Along with Fish and Wildlife, the base manages a large nature reserve of 106,110 acres within the range with cattle grazing rights that Gene Carter utilizes. The reserve, a former dune complex represents a barrier island formed during the early Pleistocene era with marine regression similar to what formed the Paleo-islands of nearby Lake Wales Ridge. Elevation on the honeycomb structure of caves, caverns, sinkhole voids in limestone, range from 40 feet along the Kissimmee River to 146 feet above mean sea level at its crest.

The APAFBR manages the 58,000-acre natural habitat of over 50 imperiled species, 40% populated by a variety of South-Central Florida vascular plants. There are seventeen specifies of frogs, turtles, reptiles, and certain identified snakes considered as a sensitive species on site. The APAFBR plays a role in protecting the regional biodiversity of one of the largest protected conservation areas in the State exceeding over a quarter million acres.

Margie Carter says in the sixty years they have lived by the range, they have never seen a crash although "we do see them bomb the targets." Gene says that leasing the land for cattle involves rotating them during the scheduled bombing practices, but "we get used to it."

As a rancher for more than forty-years, Gene conveys a practical code to live by that he passes on to the next generation of Carters: "Be honest, don't lie, and always tell the truth. Whatever you do, do the best you can. I don't know nothing about the future, but I hope all will turn out OK." As far as the present, Gene says, "You better cherish the land, agriculture, and cows as they aren't making any more land. "

Known as the City of Charm and the City of Champions Avon Park, founded in 1886, is located in the heart of Highlands County with numerous pristine lakes and old Florida woods. It was first settled in 1884 by original investor, Oliver Martin Crosby of Danbury, Connecticut and Editor of "The South" a New York publication promoting Florida worldwide. Crosby also had a quest to write about the swamps and its inhabitants of snakes, alligators, and other native reptiles. Crosby's articles attracted other adventurers to the area including a couple from England, Mr. And Mrs. William King. Mrs. King, enamored by the beauty of the wilderness suggested they re-name the town from Lake Forest to Avon Park as the beautiful, stately pines and clear lakes reminded her of her original home in Stratford-on- Avon, the birthplace of William Shakespeare.

Avon Park was incorporated as a town in 1913 and gained city status in 1925. The town gained its reputation as the "City of Champions" to honor the first high school team that won both baseball and football state championships in the same year. Avon Park is also the home of "The Downtown Mile-Long Mall" and the landmark Jacaranda Hotel in a strip of historical retail stores on old downtown Main Street.

In 2003, Highlands County had a population of 91,000; the city of Avon Park, 8,542.

THREE

"THE CATTLE BUSINESS IS BRED INTO YOU"
AVON PARK CATTLE RANCHER
GLENN MURPHY

Whether it was maneuvering through a war zone with a four star General or driving cattle across miles of Florida prairie, Glenn Murphy has and still does it all with perseverance, dedication and commitment.

"My desire to get up every morning to see if its' all still there is why I stay in the business," reflects Glenn Murphy as he looks out over his herd of registered red and Black Angus cattle that he has used genetics to breed to their "highest quality." "It's what I have done all my life." Janice Brownell, one of Joy and Glenn's grown children who Glenn says is now "the Chief," says "we like to look at good cattle."

"My grandfather bought this ranch in from the Loughton Wells family but never moved here; he raised citrus. It was my daddy, Oakley Gerald Murphy who got into the cattle business in 1945 when I was twelve years old. We started with cross-bred cattle, scrub and Brahman. I quit school in the ninth grade to work on the ranch when the screw worm epidemic came along. Then in 1951 at nineteen I was drafted into the artillery unit for a ten month duty in Korea." Although Glenn experienced a rugged young life as a cowboy, he says he wasn't prepared for the culture shock of suddenly being mobilized into very primitive circumstances. After basic training at Fort Campbell Kentucky, he was shipped out of Seattle, Washington then unloaded in from an LSU boat in the middle of the night at Inch' on, a ort on the Yellow Sea near Seoul, South Korea where the Army compound was located. "The culture shock of Korea was nothing like I had ever experienced. We were put into squad tents with refugees al around the tents begging for food." Even though early Florida pioneers were used to "outhouse," in Korea "we used boxes to sit on with a hole in it and a "caisson" with a power keg beneath it for an improvised latrine. The Korean people lived in grass huts which made me wonder why we were there. But the Korean's liked the troops." As a Florida boy used to hot sultry summers and mild winters, Murphy said the weather was another shock. "Korea had freezing temperatures and frozen ground and we had to adjust very quickly." To his credit, Murphy learned how to adapt very quickly from his early life on the Florida prairies dealing with rapidly changing weather and unexpected conditions. In Korea, as Murphy was waiting for his assignment, Major in the Army's S-3 Division needed someone to with the special ability to drive a stick-shift jeep, a skill he mastered back home. Thus, Murphy was appointed as Major Guthrie driver and self-appointed "bodyguard" as Guthrie was the point main who directed fire power. Although Murphy said he never fired a shot, as the Major's right hand man, he had to always be prepared to maneuver the Major through the war zone anywhere or anytime. Spending so much time together through very tenuous circumstances, Murphy and Guthrie got to know each other well and became good friends.

After his Korean tour, Murphy was relieved to come home to Avon Park without sustaining any injuries and to fulfill his dream of building a cattle ranch of his own. As one of five children, born in the small Polk County town of Alturas, in 1929, Murphy's early years were filled with struggle. He grew up in the Great Depression when American families were torn apart with financial destruction and often the head of families had to leave home or hitchhike on the cross-country trains to find work. Young Murphy grew through his parents divorce and continued to face whatever obstacles the family had to endure. It was his daddy's move to Avon Park that initiated young Murphy's lifelong learning to become the successful rancher that he is today. But, this dream did not manifest without hard work and determination, characteristic of Murphy.

As a teen, learning to "cowboy" ran thick in his blood; he soon mastered roping and riding and eventually those skills lured him into the rodeo arena on the weekends. He roped steers and was a steer wrestler when he was 18 years old. The rodeo opened another chapter of his life when he met Joy Hawkins his future wife when she was a flag bearer in the rodeo. The couple married June 4, 1953 and has two children, a son Del Enoch Murphy and daughter Janice Joy Brownell. Joy fell into Gene Murphy's dream of building the ranch as she had been raised in a ranching family who owned a meat packing plant. Joy was a young cow huntress and did some barrel racing in

San Mateo across the St. John's River and knew "the ropes." In 2007, the couple has been married 54 years.

The first project for the young couple was to clear the virgin land for a house which they had to do with horse and plough. "When the children came along we put Janice and Del on an old horse as a baby sitter; Janice would fall sound asleep on its back while we worked cows, said Joy. "The whole family grew up as we worked to build the ranch. We put up fences, dug watering holes and planted citrus. As young children they learned to "fetch it." When the kids were in the back of the pick up they helped by handing various tools to their parents. But the couple had fortitude, and by 1956 they were able to move into their home. Besides working at the ranch, Murphy also worked many years as the marketing agent for Deseret Citrus and Cattle Farms of Florida and was a bonded cattle broker. Today, Murphy's ranch encompasses more than twenty thousand acres including a diversification of citrus crops.

The ranching business runs in the blood as Janice and her daughter Erin are also involved in the business. Erin is earning a science degree at Brigham Young University in Idaho and Janice teaches Ag at Sebring Middle School. Her other son also works on the ranch when he is not golfing, but all the grandchildren have participated in the Highlands County Fair and 4-H clubs. Glenn is as proud of his family as they are of him. Janice says they have worked hard together on the ranch but also have a lot of laughs. Janice says she has learned to do almost everything around the ranch but is happy that "daddy keeps a good sharp edge on his knife," referring to the time when a bull has to be castrated. "He knows how to do a good "knife cut." Today,

Joy still helps out in the pens; they all wean, vaccinate, worm and weigh cattle. There isn't any general breakdown on this ranch. But the laughs are there also, like the time Del was riding a green colt and let him run wide open. But, the horse ran toward the gate and Del couldn't stop it. The horse jumped the gate as he was screaming and crying. Dell was so hot that he came back and made the horse jump the fence again.

After Gene's back surgery he rides a jeep instead of a horse around the ranch but still watches over the ranch management along with his daughter. At one time, Murphy raised quarter horses that raced at Pompano Park. And one mare, Miss High Step," ran the "Show-Me" Futurity in Illinois, but this was a hobby; the Murphy's first love is the cattle ranching.

If there are words to the wise that Murphy lives by is his belief that if you take care of the land, it will take care of you. Janice adds that she has learned about ranching by "watching daddy." Joy says that you cannot learn ranching of out of a book; it takes practical knowledge and common sense. Ranching is difficult in Central Florida. "We taught our children through hard work. When we cleared the ground we had to improve it. We taught the children to be honest and truthful and keep their word."

With an eye to the future on cattle ranching, Murphy does not believe that imported beef will hurt the Florida cattle market. But he doesn't make any predictions. "The green belt laws keep ranches in business, but there is a lot of red-tape and new regulations." Janice adds that there are also many "new people today from the outside moving into Florida that don't value agriculture." Her daddy emphasizes that "hard work is how to keep the land going" but the caveat Murphy emphasizes as a question: "Who wants to do hard work today?"

In 2006, Glenn and Joy Murphy were selected for the Hall of Fame by the Florida Cracker Trail Association. The Murphy's are member of the Church of the Latter Day Saints where Glenn holds the position as an Elder. The couple still lives at the house they built and on the land they nurtured into fruition. Their children and some grandchildren live in Avon Park.

FOUR

PIONEER "COW HUNTRESS" OF LORIDA
NELL PRESCOTT

It's hard to visualize petite, gentle woman Nell Prescott with her Southern manner and charm as a tough-hided "cow huntress," however, listening to the stories over 82 years of her life, it is clear that she stood her own along with the best of them.

Growing up in the rural prairies and palmettos of Lorida during the 1900s Depression "was not being raised in the lap of luxury," says Nell Prescott, however, it was how pioneer "cow hunters" carved a living from wild Florida. Nell's home for more than 70 years is nestled beneath arching oaks at trail's end off a rutted path where a red-eared turtle lays its eggs unperturbed by time or occasional traffic. Although Nell says her horseback riding days are over, on occasion she uses her golf cart to drive back a stray cow heading for the highway. "I saw that a steer had gotten through the fence, so I herded him back to the pasture, but that rascal got out again. This time I made a bunch of racket and scared him away from the road.

My nephews, Mike and Quinn Ashton, came by later and fixed the fence, but you know, cows are not as dumb as people make them, if they know where they can get through a fence, they will come back to that spot again and try to get out."

Iva Bass, Nell's mother, the youngest of nine children, was born in Whittier now Kenansville, Florida and passed on in 1997 at the age 103. Iva met and married Rudy Ashton in 1919; he was born east of St. Cloud. They had three children: Ruby born in Kissimmee in 1921, Nell, born in 1925, and Miles (nicknamed "Babe") born in 1927. After Ruby was in the seventh grade, "we moved to Lorida from Avon Park but we had to rent an apartment in downtown Sebring to go to school, as there was no bus to pick us up in the sticks." Nell says they were proud that Ruby graduated as Valedictorian from Sebring High School since "Miles and I were not the intellectual types and would rather have a good time than study!"

Adapting to rural conditions over a lifetime and growing up during the Great Depression instilled in Nell a keen awareness of "change." "I grew up on dirt roads with kerosene lamps, a wood stove, and no running water; we had to carry a bucket up to the house. Today, there are paved roads, electricity, and satellite TVs. In the cow business, we went from scrub cattle raised in palmetto woods to 'blooded' [bred-up] cattle raised on improved pasture. All of these things have made life more comfortable and manageable but I enjoyed those yesteryears and learned to be happy with what I had, not wanting those things we couldn't afford. This still applies today."

"When I was eight years old, we didn't have things but daddy had a job, we had food, clothes, and a roof over our heads (even though it leaked), and we never went to bed hungry. We grew potatoes, peas, and other vegetables and Mamma canned them; it wasn't gourmet food but it stuck to our ribs. Mamma, like other wives of that era, stayed at home seeing to her family's needs. She washed on a rub board, ironed with a flat iron heated on a wood stove; she even ironed the sheets and pillow cases besides cooking three meals a day. She used hog lard and bacon grease for frying and baking. Meals consisted mostly of meat, dry beans or black-eyed peas, rice, tomato gravy, cornbread or biscuits, milk, butter and syrup. These were the staples." With a sense of humor the way Nell tells it, "the wood stove cooked all the calories, cholesterol, and triglycerides out of the food. We never went without medical attention and went to the doctor if we needed to not just for sympathy." With only a few settlers living miles apart and a doctor just as far, families had to learn to how to treat themselves with basic provisions and applications. "We boiled kerosene for sprains, used castor oil, Epson salt, B.C. headache powder, and Lysol for disinfectant." It was the way of life.

In those early no frills days, Nell says "there wasn't any candy on the table or sodas to drink, but we survived and I never knew we were in 'bad times.' Everyone said it was 'hard times' because you couldn't get things and the cost of everything was so high. But even after the war, some products were still high, so I don't know if we were worse or better off then, as I'm still hearing the same thing today. It's true costs are higher but we have to accept it. The one big difference is that now you can borrow money to buy things using credit cards. All of this can be the ruination of a person if they don't control their spending. When you max out a credit card you can sure be in trouble. Growing up in the Depression taught me 'to appreciate' and to be resourceful. I enjoy all the modern day conveniences but I miss the closeness we had in the community during those days, but life goes on, change takes place, and we have to adjust."

Nell's daddy earned a living as a "cow hunter," following the cattle where there was a job. In 1933, Rudy was hired by Lykes Brothers to oversee the cattle range of Lorida from Lake Istokpoga to the Kissimmee River including the Avon Park Bombing Range. "'Cow hunters' back then didn't have the luxury of trucks and trailers, so they camped at the cow pens where they were working. There was one shelter at Scrub Pens, six miles north of Lorida, and later one was built at Hickory Hammock on the Kissimmee River, otherwise there was no shelter."

The 'cow hunters' were rugged and adaptable. They learned the way of the land and the cattle, and became part of Nature in which they lived. Nell says it was a "hard life with rain the norm for the day." At night when there were torrential downpours, the men would break out their slickers, if they had one, to endure thunder and lighting, hoping not to be in the line of a deadly strike; then they had to settle down again into sopping wet bedding that might never dry out before the next downpour. This is how "they put food on the table for their families and they should be commended for facing such hardships."

Eventually, Nell's daddy was able to buy and lease some land of his own, "he bought a bull dozer to clean up the swamp and some other equipment for haymaking. My daddy was always looking ahead. He was progressive and self-confident. He had an attitude of 'I can do it.' He always said the word 'can't' should not be used, you were defeated before starting, if that was your mindset."

As a young cow "huntress," Nell learned to work alongside her daddy at the young age of eleven besides Miles, who was nine. "Once we were driving some cattle alongside a barb wire fence with thunder and lightning popping all around us. I was next to the fence. Miles rode over to me and said 'Nell, let me get here next to the fence, if the lighting strikes that fence, it could kill you.' Those kinds of memories are a lifetime."

The family also worked as a unit to combat the screw worm epidemic that Nell says "was one of the most damaging things to ever happen to the livestock industry. Any wound, especially in the navels of newborn calves, got infected when the fly burrowed its eggs into the soft flesh, then maggots hatched that eventually fell out and became more flies. Any infected animal had to be roped and doctored with 'Smear X,' a black tar-like medicine that would seal off the wound and suffocate the maggots. Daddy would rope the grown animals, run ahead and bust them (or trip them and they would fall). I'd jump off my horse, pull the cow's tail up in her flank and hold her down while he doctored it. To turn her loose, Daddy put the rope over her two hind feet, stretched her out, and I'd get on my horse. Then he slacked the rope and she'd kick it off. We sometimes did have a few cows that would not let you doctor their calves. They would stand over the calf and if you got up there to them, they would run into you and hook your horse." Nell wasn't much for roping, she says, but she could bust a cow and doctor it with help. "In my lifetime, I've seen the eradication of fever ticks, screw worms, and brucellosis, now I want to see the same come about for soda apples, fire ants, love bugs, and our armed forces brought home out of a place they should never have been sent."

In 1933, Rudy bought the family a house and ten acres in Lorida for $50.00, later "trading 20 acres in Avon Park for 20 acres here; it was his last move. This is where he lived and he died. My nephew now owns the land so it's still in the family."

There were many close calls in the wilderness as "cow hunters" were confronted with unpredictable situations that had to be handled with ingenuity; "so many of them were comical that the general public doesn't know about," recalls Nell. "One time three miles away from a crevice, we found a Brahman bull that stayed off to himself. There was no cattle around to drive him but Daddy wanted to bring him in to sell. We began pushing him along real easy with no trouble for awhile, then he started 'bowing up' and began to fight. Daddy took his rope down and said, 'I'll rope him, you tie on with me, and we'll take him in.' In the meantime, the bull tried to hook my horse. I said, 'No, daddy, I won't do that.' He kept telling me, 'You can do it, come on now and help me.' When he started toward the bull with his rope, I said 'OK, I'm going home, good-bye!' He called out to wait, and went over to a broken fence post. I turned back just in time to see daddy sail the old fence post right between the bull's eye. With that lick, the bull turned and we drove him in."

"The next day, we were riding horses to move some cows when we came across a man whose tractor got stuck in boggy ground and he couldn't get it loose. Daddy put his rope over the plow to pull it away from the tractor, but when he tightened it, his girth broke and he took a spill. I said, 'See daddy what could have happened yesterday?'"

"My daddy was a legendary, one-of-a-kind person. He was straight forward, said what he thought and meant what he said. He wasn't diplomatic, he told you 'flat-out.' He always said: 'The only time it was all right to tell a lie was to keep somebody from beating hell out of you, then it's OK to lie, but that's the only time. Otherwise, tell the truth!'"

As the country prepared for wartime during the early 40's, there was a teacher shortage. Nell had always been interested in becoming a teacher so after high school she enrolled in a summer education course at Florida Southern University to attain her teaching certificate. In the Fall of 1943, she received her first position at Sunnyland School in Lorida teaching a combined class of third and fourth graders. There were four teachers, teaching first through eighth grade, in the little four room school house. For the next two years, Nell taught first, second, and third graders. "There was a desk in the front and benches. Each class was in a different row and each would come to the front for instruction while the other students worked on what they had been given to do. There were no discipline problems, the students minded well. I had about twenty to twenty-five students."

In the 50's, Nell took a position at the tax collector's office in Sebring where she met M.F. Prescott, a retired Navy veteran from Sebring, soon-to-be her husband. They married in 1960 when Nell was 34 and M.F. 40. M.F. Prescott was a man known around the community for his strength and service. M.F. Prescott was described by the First Baptist Minister, Marcus Marshall, as a man "you could count on. The way he carried himself, his stature, and his personality were some of his strengths. When he made a commitment to do something, he carried it out to the fullest." Nell says that "all his life he loved livestock but because of his Navy career, he was unable to be in the cattle business until after retiring.

If there is one major concern that Nell expresses, it is about the future of the small family ranch due to many new regulations and large inheritance taxes. "The cattle business is unpredictable. Regulations and environmentalists are necessary in a practical sense, but many rules are imposed on ranchers in a whim, by people in power with no hands-on knowledge. They come up with costly regulations to be 'tried' and the rancher has to comply at his expense. If it doesn't work, who is the loser?" Additionally, large inheritance taxes threaten the continuation of the small family ranch to stay in business, "slapping a 50% tax of the appraised value to be paid by heirs on property that has been in a family for years, when the owners want to pass it to heirs to continue operating as a ranch. Most likely heirs will have to borrow money to pay the tax so the next generation inherits the burden and the cycle starts all over again, unless laws are changed. It seems unfair that heirs should have to buy back something they want to continue." Nell proclaims that she is not "smart enough to know how to make laws," but says "if a small ranch is to continue with the heirs, a one time tax on the year of death of the gross income for that year, would be fair. Now, future taxes are paid on income and heirs also have to pay off any money borrowed to pay the inheritance tax. This, in turn, can cause the sale of land for development. For the next generations, I can see how they would rather go into another profession with better pay, benefits, and regular hours rather than fight the fight. In ranching, you can be a millionaire on paper and have to borrow money to pay your bills. Costs of cattle raising are unseen by people on the outside. All they see is the land, cattle, and the check when you sell the cattle at the market, not how long you waited for that check and the cost in-between. It can be a long, dry spell before sale day and the 'take back [or "repo"] man' can be there waiting on his pay. A person today cannot, with land and prices what they are, borrow money to buy land and raise cattle; the interest alone would eat you up. Many negatives go along with ranching but the positives outnumber the negatives to people who have spent a lifetime in the business. To paraphrase an old saying: 'Old ranchers don't retire, they just fade away.' Most ranchers are good stewards of their land; they know the land by taking care of it, it will in turn take care of them. Learning is by trial and error, and being cautious before jeopardizing holdings. You have challenges, frustrations, and disappointments but the love of your work and accomplishments puts all those negatives in the background."

Although Nell and M.F. did not have children of their own, they have "a passel of nieces and nephews, all seven of them living in the community. No mother ever had children to treat her any better than these do me. I have been spoiled by my husband and all the family. One by one, Daddy, Miles, M.F., Mamma and Ruby have passed away. I miss them but you can't live in the past. Life goes on. Live today and recall happy memories. I'm thankful for the good life I still enjoy, the big and little things that come my way. By putting God first, everything else falls into place and I'm blessed and happy. Being a Florida cracker and living here in Lorida seventy-four years, I have no desire to live anywhere else. This community has been good to me and my family. In my way of thinking, it's the 'bestest.' If it isn't, don't tell me because I won't believe you. As the lady with the black eye in the TV commercial says, 'I'd rather fight than switch.'"

In the meantime, surrounded by pastures, native scrub, nearby Arbuckle Creek between miles of open prairie, Nell Prescott continues to enjoy a way of life she has always known in a community that knows her, and remains unspoiled by urban influences moving up and down U.S. Highway 27 a few miles west. Lorida is a town that greets travelers with a welcome sign on Highway 98 marking its entrance on both ends. A church, post office, grocery store, gas station, mom and pop businesses, and the restored school house where Nell taught, reside along the roadside in this quiet unincorporated community in Highlands County, named for the high terrain in the area. The little village of Lorida got its name in the 1900s when present day Highlands County Commissioner Edgar Stokes' Postmaster mother took the "F" off of "Florida" to name the town, not confuse the local mail delivery with the state's namesake.

Highlands County population from the 2000 Census: 87,366; estimated population of Lorida: 1,646.

FIVE

"WALKING BESIDE MY TANK, I STOPPED TO CHECK TANK TRACKS WHEN A MARINE SHOUTED: 'LOOK OUT OVER THERE....'"

ON THE STARK VOLCANIC ROCK OF MT. SURIBACHI DURING WORLD WAR II, THE AMERICAN FLAG WAS HOISTED,"....AND THEN WE KEPT ON FIGHTIN'."

DUCK SMITH, UNITED STATES MARINE AND MYAKKA "COW HUNTER" NORMAN PROVEAUX, KEN MCLEOD

"Although we were very poor, I came up in the best world I've ever seen. When people ask me about growing up in the Depression, I say, 'you can't comprehend it,'" reflects Norman Proveaux born in 1924 "way back in the woods southwest of Fort Green between Highway 62 and 64." Norman Proveaux is a World War II Veteran and "cow hunter" who lived through events archived in Florida and United States history.

Traveling through the backwoods over one dirt road after another is like venturing into another era when "cow hunters," their horses, and dogs carved trails through Manatee, Desoto, Sarasota, Hillsborough, and Hardee Counties across Highway 27, living by their keen sense of the land that gave them food and a livelihood. Today, a devout Christian, Proveaux admits that "it wasn't always my way of life until one day my eight year old daughter, Glenda, wanted me to go to church. I said, 'No I have to go to work.' She stood firm and said, 'Well then, Daddy, just go to hell and see if I care!' I gave this some thought and decided I would go and become a Christian." Proveaux acknowledges his belief that "God is his source of strength and direction. It doesn't matter what faith you are, there is a God who determines what will happen."

At a young age, harsh and difficult times were a way of life. In the 1800s, Proveaux's parents traveled from Waldenberg, South Carolina to settle in the back woods southwest of Fort Green, the land was raw, untamed and "everyone was poor. The family grew ten children and adopted two others who were rescued into the family. "Pa found a young black girl and her baby living under a tree." He brought them back to take care of and who, over their lifetime, took care of them.

"Many people in the 30s lost their land because they couldn't pay the taxes," reminisces Proveaux. "It wasn't until I was about six years old that I got my first new pair of britches. I started cow hunting when I was twelve years old," he says. During those times, manual labor and ingenuity was the only way to survive. "If you didn't grow a garden, you couldn't live," he adds. The workhorse was attached to a hand-made wooden plough used to cultivate a garden. Most everyone lived off the land except for some of the rich landowners that "looked down on those with lesser means," says Proveaux. He recalls one such incident that changed forever his political view. "I will never again vote Republican because of what happened with this one man who owned land on both sides of the Manatee River. We were down on our knees with axes and 'grubben' hoes [a wooden handled tool with a cupped iron "spoon" on the end to tug up and cut palmetto roots] clearing five acres to grow peas, when this man and his three servants rode up to us. He was hateful. Ma [respectfully called 'Miss Janie' by friends] and my three sisters had brought down some dinner on the horse wagon about a mile from the house. Ma invited the man to dinner but he didn't want to eat. Then he asked my Ma if she was a Republican or Democrat. Ma asked him, 'What did that have to do with planting peas?' He said, 'Well, if you were a Republican you'd have servants behind you like me and you wouldn't have to do work like this.'"

"First my brother Bubba, who was a large man, headed for him. Ma, who was only four foot, eleven inches did not say a word but pointed her finger at the wagon; Bubba stopped in his tracks. Then my other two brothers started after the man. Ma again pointed her finger at the wagon again. My brothers backed off and the man moved on. There were a lot of Northerners who came to Florida and bought land but not all of them were like this man. One group of about fifteen families settled off of County Road 675 towards Parrish and started the town of 'Manhattan.' They were real nice folks. It was around 1929 that Mr. and Mrs. Kidder bought me the first pair of new overalls I ever had in my life."

Norman Proveaux's daddy was a "cow hunter" and "range rider" for the turpentine company in the late 1800-1900s. The range rider's job was to check on workers and keep the peace. Northerners, who came to Florida in the early days, bought up vast sections of timber land to harvest turpentine used for many purposes including medicinal.

Ken McLeod, a good friend of Susan and Duck Smith, owners of the Bar Crescent S Ranch in Wauchula, worked many years as Cow-Foreman for Susan's daddy, Doyle Carlton, Jr. and her granddaddy Doyle Carlton, Sr. former Governor of Florida, 1929-33. McLeod describes another early development in a huge virgin pine area south of Arcadia and southwest of Wauchula on Highway 31 called "Del Verde." "Many years ago when I worked cows for H.P. Wright, I used to drive them across the overgrown sidewalks in this platted community. They built a shirt factory and huge Spanish mansions that later mysteriously burned down." Florida's history is replete with developments that became dust in the wind during the 1900 "boom days" before the Great Depression. McLeod and Smith are long-time friends of the Proveauxs' and visit them often.

Hunting down cattle through miles of rugged terrain was a way of life for pioneer "cow hunters" with long days "starting at 4:30 a.m. until long after dark, during the dipping days of the 30's," says Proveaux. "Since we had no electricity or water, my mama got up and cooked biscuits stuffed with onions and potatoes that she made before daybreak by the light of a kerosene lantern. Then she read her Bible aloud one hour every morning. I wasn't a Christian then, but the way she read the Bible, I could visualize every word."

Some of the land around Proveaux's ranch, according to Smith and McLeod is "just land that holds the world together. The land is not fit for cattle as it is weak," says Smith referring to the sandy scrub interlaced with miles of thick and spiky palmettos. Rounding up cattle for Proveaux in this dense prairie with his "jip" cur dog, "Anne" at his heel, meant maneuvering through the rugged underbrush to rope and root out the herd. Since there were no fence laws until the 40's, the cracker cattle were wild, and "they would lay down and hide in a bunch of palmettos. You had to find them first before you could get them out. It was hard work," Proveaux explains, reliving those times. A "cow hunter" in the old days, stayed out with the cows for months at a time," working for various ranchers.

When out in the woods, "I picked up dried cow dung and moss for a fire that smoked mosquitoes away." Proveaux traveled the range with a couple of horses and cur dogs "as far south as Ft. Myers, north to Tampa and west to about where Highway 27 is today." When Duck Smith, Ken McLeod and Norman Proveaux were gathered together in Proveaux's old barn at his ranch in Myakka looking over an old wooden pair of McClellan stirrups long retired and hanging in memory, Smith recalls a story Proveaux told him about those early days. "Norman said his brother sent him in the mail, a bonafide 'Boney-Allen' tree saddle. Even though it was 'used,' he was real excited about getting it because it had a horn to tie his rope onto and sat better than the 'McClellan Tree' with the split down the middle. The 'Boney-Allen' tree saddle was one of the first western-type saddles to be used by cowboys; I know they have been around for a long time. However, after receiving the 'Boney-Allen' saddle, Proveaux threw the 'McClellan' saddle in a palmetto patch and set fire to it because of all the saddle sores and bruises he received. In other words, he grew to despise it, but it was a necessary evil if he was going to be a 'cow hunter' riding horses during this time in history. Reflecting much later on what he did, Proveaux told Ken and I that he 'wished he hadn't of done it.' You had to be a "tough knocker" to survive that kind of life that he and other like-kinds endured in the early days of the cattle industry here in Florida."

"We read and hear about the cowboys and cowmen out West," adds Smith, "but the 'cow hunters' and cowmen of Florida were just as real, ornery, and authentic as they were in the West. They probably started herding cattle here in Florida before they did in the western states because the Spanish explorers and colonists brought the little Spanish cattle into Florida before they hit Mexico and Texas." Proveaux gave a pair of his old McClellan stirrups to

Duck Smith where they abide today on the mantle of his Wauchula ranch cabin alongside other "cow hunter" memorabilia.

George B. McClellan developed the McClellan Tree Saddle over many years. Its origin dates back to the Crimean War where McClellan served as a Captain, using different types of foreign made military equipment, suggesting updates to the Army. In the 19th Century, the military was evaluating several styles of saddles including the "Jones Adjustable Tree Saddle," the "Hope," the standard service "Grimsley," the flexible "Campbell," and the new style  Captain McClellan offered. It is believed that the McClellan saddle was selected due to is practical cost and serviceability. General McClellan led Union forces against Jefferson Davis' Rebels in what was called "the Southern War of Independence (Civil War).

When Proveaux was a teenager, World War II began. "I was working a pile of cattle on U.S. 41 which is 'South Gate' today in Sarasota. It was Sunday, December 7, 1941, when a Model A, working its way through the cattle, pulled up with a woman inside crying. I overheard her say that Pearl Harbor had been bombed. I didn't know anything about it, so I asked another rider, 'Slim,' 'What was Pearl Harbor?' He looked up and down at the ground, and looked up and down at the ground again, and said, 'I don't know.' We looked for Mr. Van, about 80 years old who was our Foreman, to ask him about this. We got over there to him and he said, 'You are out of place!' I said, 'I got to ask you something. What is Pearl Harbor?' Mr. Van said it was a naval port in the Hawaiian Islands. 'Why are you asking?' I said, 'It has been bombed.' All Mr. Van said was, 'Oh my gracious!' As I went to ride away back to the herd, Mr. Van said, 'this will change your life forever, son!' I said, 'No sir, it can't affect me.' Mr. Van replied, 'Yes, son, it will.' About a year later, I lied about my age and joined the Marines. We trained at Paris Island for eight weeks and were shipped out to the front lines on Iwo Jima."

According to historical records, Iwo Jima was a small island administered by the government in Tokyo. In 1943, the island had a civilian population of 1,018 and 192 households. There was a primary school, a Shinto shrine, and a single police officer. The island's economy relied upon sulfur mining, sugarcane, and fishing. It is said to have been a poor island in the middle of the Pacific Ocean.

"Why did I join the Marines? When the war broke out our military was very weak, we were whipped. Our Lieutenant, a boy from Mississippi, took good care of us. When I got there, Lieutenant Miledge came over and asked me if I knew how to drive a Mac Hendry. I said I had never driven anything, I was a 'cow hunter' and had only driven cattle. He said, 'Well, go over there to that tank.' So that was my job. It was our Lieutenant Miledge, about 22, not much older than me, who gave us great inspiration; he was a Christian. He gave everyone courage. He always said: 'Be yourself, don't say that nothing bothers you, we are all scared.'"

"In one of the many invasions there was a Chaplin who traveled with some leathernecks (we called them) or foot troops. In the *Leatherneck Magazine* there was a story I remember about a Chaplin. As the Chaplin looked out over innocent faces of young Marines, one kid smiled and said to everyone who could hear him, 'cheer up, the Chaplin's not scared!' It was this young boy's faith that carried the Chaplin through the war."

Those grueling days to capture the volcanic island, 1,200 kilometers south of mainland Tokyo at the southern end of the Ogasawara Islands, was where the "Battle of Imo Jima" occurred. "It was an every day life or death situation," says Proveaux. He received more injuries as a Marine then wounds he received as a "cow hunter." Young Proveaux and his 4th Division of Marines fought endlessly on the stark naked island marked by a rugged, craggy peak Mt. Suribachi, rising from the center of the submerged caldera. It was on a rocky military road beneath the volcano where Proveaux and his Marine tank troop witnessed an extraordinary event carved in the minds of all Americans and depicted in the bronze monument at Paris Island. It was the raising of the American flag on Mt. Suribachi.

"This day was just like every other weary one during the war," says Proveaux, as exhausted troops traipsed across the battlefield beside their tanks. Proveaux describes the experience as if it were yesterday. "The gunner was peering out of the tank top then started shouting and pointing, 'look out over there!' When someone starts shouting, 'look out,' everyone prepares for battle." But, the young gunner was pointing to a phenomenal event as the 5th Marine Division hoisted the American flag atop Mount Suribachi. "And then we kept on fighting," added Proveaux, "Nothing stopped." On the chiseled peak of Mt. Suribachi, the red, white, and blue braced the wind over charred bodies of young soldiers who gave their lives for their country.

War leaves mental, physical, and psychological scars. Norman Proveaux doesn't talk about the horrors he experienced but remembers humorous moments, "if there were any," he says. In one incident, Proveaux met a "short man in a black suit who was visiting the 4th Marine Division walking up and down the ranks, shaking hands with troops. The man came over to where my tank was and said, 'hello, Marine, my name is President Harry Truman.' I spoke back real quick because I didn't believe he was the President of the United States, and said, 'Well, hello, my name is Jack Dempsey and I'm the Heavyweight Champion of the World!"

"One time I came back to get some fifty M.O. caliber for our guns and fuel when I noticed, not too far away, someone had welded together some barrels for a latrine over volcanic lava. The Lieutenant and I were sitting on the boards when suddenly a bunch of Japanese opened fire on us. We didn't take time to pull up our britches but dove! Afterwards, we didn't see the Lieutenant and I thought, 'they got him.' We looked all over for him. Then this big, tall man comes straddling out of the latrine. I told him, 'I would never have done that!' Lieutenant Mildege was a Christian, but he said, 'Gator, I'd rather be alive and crappy, then dead and not!"

"This never came out, but we heard that the Japanese had loaded troops to invade the west coast of the U.S. but got lost. The Japanese had taken the Philippines and were planning to take Australia. Every man was enlisting. I think the turning point was Guadalcanal."

According to "Restricted" data from an address by Rear Admiral H.R. Thurber, USN, Director of Logistic Planning published by the Industrial College of the Armed Forces, November 1950 and released as part of the Freedom of Information Act, Thurber's comments reinforce Proveaux's belief about Guadalcanal.

> "In the "critical stage of the Guadalcanal fight which lasted until 15 November 1942, the enemy tried by every means to sever our supply line. On five different nights a strong group of Japanese surface vessels attempted to reinforce and recapture Guadalcanal. Invariably, these outnumbered the only surface vessels with which we could oppose them. We succeeded each time in obstructing their attempts to recapture the islands; but had they on any one occasion destroyed our naval forces, then the thin thread of supply would have been severed permanently, and the Guadalcanal position would have been lost."

'When I was getting ready to return to the U.S. in 1946, the Lieutenant said to me, "Gator, (they called me that because I was from Florida), what are you going to do after you get home?' I said I was going to do what I always had done, go back to cow hunting. I asked him what he was going to do and he said, 'I ain't going to raise no more families.'"

"After the war I was worn out   I went in as a private and came out as a private. I got $21 a month as an enlisted man and when I came out I got the same but with the war going on there weren't many 'cow hunters' left back home. One day Mr. Wiles Harrison came to the house and said he wanted me to start 'screw wormin'' again. I said, 'No sir!' He said, 'I'll give you $5.00 a day.' I told him, 'I'll start tomorrow!' I had never made $5.00 a day in my life. We spent three or four days at Waterbury, near County Road 675 between State Road 64 and 70, where we bedded down at the cow pens by a little old shed. While I was working cows, all I could think about was this blue-eyed girl from high school who always smiled. One night I just got up around 1 a.m. and left with my two horses and dog. I got home by daylight and walked to Bradenton to borrow my brother's car. I thought Joyce, that is her name, was at Bradenton High School. I got in the old Pontiac that my brother told me would not start again if it got hot, but made it anyway to school. I saw her but there were too many girls around. I was scared of girls. I went on back to the car but it wouldn't start. So I sat there. Then I saw her with three other girls going to the Bethany bus. I eased back on over there and called her name. She knew me. I told her a lie and said I had come looking for someone else (she believed me). Later she found out that wasn't true. I drove the twenty-five miles to Bethany. A few months later on July 20, 1946, we were married. Afterwards, we went home and had to keep right on working. There was no honeymoon but God gave me a perfect wife. We have been married 61 years."

Ken McLeod, Susan and Duck Smith

Today, "cow hunters" like "Duck" Smith and Ken McLeod still gather cattle and raise horses, although Ken says he is retired. Times have changed in the cattle business, according to Smith and McLeod. "Cattlemen are 'ranchers,' and 'cow hunters,' who are the ones that go into the field, and 'cow men' mostly manage the ranch and do some of both." One time Proveaux said his nephew asked him, "How come you weren't never a cowboy?" Proveaux says he never heard the term "cowboy" until after he returned from the war. Duck Smith said the term "'cowboy' originated during the Civil War when men were away fighting and young boys were hired to drive cattle on the long cross-state trails to the rail heads."

Nevertheless, bumping along the rutted dirt roads carved by those who came

before but in a 4 x 4 pick-up with Ken McCloud and "Duck" Smith on the way to Norman Proveaux's ranch, there is no doubt that the pioneer "cow hunter" spirit is the lifeblood of these ranchers. Despite the technological evolution of modern day ranching, Smith and McLeod preserve the old-fashioned gentlemanly ways and timeless traditions of pioneer "cow hunter" Norman Proveaux's era in history.

The little town of Myakka where Norman and Joyce Proveaux's ranch is nestled in the woods, is located in a remote southeast corner of Manatee County. According to the U.S. Census, population of Manatee County: 313,298; population of Myakka: not listed.

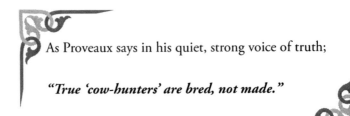

As Proveaux says in his quiet, strong voice of truth;

"True 'cow-hunters' are bred, not made."

SIX

"IF A MAN'S WORD WAS NO GOOD, THE PAPER HE WROTE IT ON WAS NOT ANY GOOD EITHER,"

RALEIGH ORMOND SIMMONS AND THE "COW HUNTER CONCLAVE"

Every Wednesday, on the outskirts of Orlando (East Orange County) at Al

Johnson's "cowboy condo" (an open barn with long wooden benches on a dust floor), the "Cow Hunter Conclave" meets for a fresh brew of coffee and pot luck to talk about the "good old days" with the pioneers who lived it.

Gathering together at 9:00 a.m., the regulars greet each other and sit down in their regular places as Al Johnson, Wade and Mindi Reddit, (son and daughter-in-law of pioneer cow hunter Willard Reddit) pass around the home made goodies. A lively discussion begins when Sheriff's Deputy Bill Meeks dropped by just long enough to endure some "inside razing," retorting with the quip, "If you're going to be dumb, you'd better be tough!" As the group settled down, the new book published by the Christmas, Florida historical society, *Fort Christmas A Pictorial History,* was passed around. The book depicts, in pictures and text, histories of pioneer families who first settled the nearby community in the 1800s. The anointed "Mayor of Christmas" Charles Yates, 72, was on hand to sign a copy as well as others in the book.

The order of the day was lively talk weaving through memories and time, far removed from the experience of newcomers to the area who are settling in the urban Orlando area. However, as the pioneers begin to tell their personal stories, it awakens the past and history becomes a living testimony.

When early 1800s settlers trekked to Florida by horse, wagon, boat, or on foot, the environment was not easily adaptable. They had to machete through miles of palmetto thickets, tall grasses, trudging through marshes and sloughs; yet for cattle raising, the land was prime. For those who first set out in lighter boats on the northward flowing St. Johns River, they discovered its rich alluvial plains sprawling from the banks with the lure of good hunting and farming. With no fence laws until a hundred years later, wild scrawny scrub cattle left by 1500s Spanish explorers were rounded up on the range by "cow hunters" and over time, bred into quality herds. As more ranchers settled in Florida, they got together twice a year for round ups to herd thousands of cattle across the state to market. One cow-hunter who rode those old "cracker trails" and tells it like it was, is Raleigh Ormond Simmons, 90.

Since he was eight years old, Simmons worked around the St. Johns River cutting cabbage palms and "cow hunting." "During World War II, muzzle loaded guns used cabbage palm leaves for 'wading.' You first put powder in the muzzle, the shot, and then wading," says Simmons. "Wading was used before closed casings. Simmons was born in 1917 north of Titusville at LaGrange, where the St. Johns River goes on its way south. He grew up with his five sisters and brother on his Uncle Irving Simmons' ranch who migrated to Florida from South Carolina. "As a boy, Uncle Irving furnished us meals and we butchered cattle for the little Titusville market. We all went barefoot and made boar hair brushes as it stood up stiff. As far as schooling, I went through part of the ninth grade at Oveida High School."

"In those days, we all helped each other out with two or three families working together. Most ranchers did not see each other for six or eight months, then we all got together on a certain date on the prairie to gather wild horses off the marshes or cows east and west of the St. Johns to Mims, north of Titusville. We met on two dates during the year and brought five or six wagonloads of camping supplies for a big picnic on the river. We got all the fish we needed and threw the rest back. Everyone was there. Daddy had a big lot to hold cattle where we branded and ear-marked loose cows. Sometimes there were hundreds. If a cow strayed from the bunch and it was branded, the honest man did not keep him."

In wild Florida, the pages of history are flawed with lawlessness that settlers had to face, sometimes with their own measure of justice. As Simmons tells it, "rustlers would steal cattle then draw their own brand over others." An act of cattle thievery was dealt with harshly. "The cure for cattle rustling, in those days, was a shotgun filled with buckshot. In Palmdale [Glades County] there were three fellas rustling cattle who were mysteriously killed when they stopped to open a gate. If a cattle rustler was caught by the law, they were hung or did jail time. Evidence of cattle rustling turned up in gator caves where only the hides were found."

Willard Reddit, another local pioneer from Conway, recalls a cattle rustling incident when he worked at a meatpacking plant. "Some men came in with meat but no hides; they had to have the hides or the brand inspector was called in." Ed Yates added that "they found people out by the airport with a whole backyard full of buried hides."

Traditionally, "cattle branding was a family affair," Simmons explained. "A wife and husband each had their own brand as well as the children. If a wife's heifer had a calf, sometimes a husband would not let them brand the calf until the next year then he might just put his own brand on it." Many ranchers in Florida did cut their cattle a "dew lap" as a brand, but most used ear marks, as is still practiced today.

Although the hardy young "cow hunters" worked many long hours in scorching temperatures, hail storms, and freezing weather on dusty prairies, they somehow found time for mischief, "sparking," and marriage. "Sometimes for fun as school boys, we put a 12 gauge shotgun shell on the stove until it got hot and then put it on one of the other boy's backsides. Why did we do it, because we could." As a youth, Ormond was a prankster. His spunk still endures in his wiry sense of humor and stealth in storytelling, sometimes "trapping" an intent listener that consequently results in a round of laughter from those "in the know" when the unsuspecting bites the bait. In another memorable prank, Simmons recalls the "sulfur doodle" incident. "When we worked for Mann Bailey, who managed cattle around the St. Johns River, a new boy, Bud Hagen from Wildwood joined us. He was not familiar with the area and we always 'hazed' new 'cow hunters.' Around the river there are places called 'sulfur doodles,' or a hole with quicksand. We rode lots of times alongside a 'sulfur doodle' but you can't see them as grass grows over it. Cattle go along the edge and stick their front legs in to feed on grass. Since Hagen was new, one old boy dared another to ride him into the 'sulfur doodle.' We all came along side him on our horses making a circle on the flood plain around the 'sulfur doodle.' Our boss hollered to Bud, 'Get up here!' Then, some of the others managed a distraction. I rode so close by him that I reckon he thought I wanted to kiss him! Then his horse went down and kicked Bud's foot which sent him sailing, head first, into the 'sulfur doodle.'" Willard Reddit, who was also on the cow crew, laughed when he described how "Bud was holding his feet up with his right foot caught in the stirrup, the horse was down, and the cows were coming!"

Besides cutting cabbage palms, cow hunting, and pulling pranks, Simmons found time for "sparking," interpreted by Al Johnson as "necking" or "when the sparks are flying." Through "sparking," Simmons got to know his high school sweetheart, Lavonda Hickson, whom he married. After the twenty year marriage ended in divorce, Simmons married again in 1970 to Emma Lou Hazelief, the daughter of a preacher. He has been married 37 years and has six children, three born in the hospital and three by midwife Alma. Alma, the Aunt of the "Mayor of Christmas" Charles Yates, delivered most of the children in the community.

According to the chronicles in *Fort Christmas A Pictorial History*, the Yates family dates back to the 1800s. William Burrell Yates was a farmer and Minster who settled around Duval County when he left Georgia. John Burrell Yates was born in Osceola County and moved near Fort Christmas, one of the early forts Zachary Taylor constructed during the Seminole Indian

Wars. Fort Christmas was completed in December 1837. A replica of the old fort is open to the public at the Fort Christmas Historical Park. The little cracker house of Bud and Polly Yates built in 1902 and known as "the "Yates house," has been re-located to the Pioneer Homes section at the park. The Yates' raised cattle and citrus, a tradition continued by family members who still ranch and reside in the Christmas community. Christmas, west of the St. Johns River, near Titusville and Orlando is renowned by people all over the world who send tons of Christmas mail to the little post office to be postmarked: "Christmas, Florida."

Some of the early cattle people around the St. Johns River included the "McCrory's, who owned a plantation in Osceola County that provided "quality hunting," says Simmons. "In the 1940's, the Mormons came to Florida and bought part of the McCrory land which is the Deseret Ranch today." It is the largest ranch in the United States covering almost 300,000 acres with 44,000 head of cattle spreading through parts of Orange, Brevard, and Osceola counties. "The McCrory's were known in Florida for their chain of McCrory Dime Stores," Simmons adds.

As time moved forward from driving cattle to driving a Model A or T, Simmons says "my daddy had one which brings to mind some more stories." Willard Reddit said he also recalls some of his experiences with the new fangled "tin lizzie." One afternoon Reddit was cruising along over a bridge in his Model T when it stalled. "I got out and cranked it up then jumped up on down on the running board to get it started. When it did get going it wouldn't stop and headed on its own into the scrub until it stalled again. It was a pretty basic car with just three gears: reverse, stop, and forward but it did get up to about 40 mph." In another incident, Reddit says he was stranded on a pitch black night with only the light of a full moon. "The car wouldn't work because a little clip had fallen apart and off. I didn't have a flashlight but I did have one or two matches. With a full moon I could see enough to look around for some lighter wood [old pine] to light a fire so I could find out what was wrong the car. I couldn't see enough to solve that problem but I did see another one, a big old rattle snake!"

The snake moved on as Reddit was determined to fix the car or spend the night in it. Since he was eight or nine years old, he always wore a Stetson when working cows that has a band around it above the brim. Trying to figure out a way to fix the broken clips, Reddit took his hat off and cut the band to see if he could feel around the motor and tie off the clips. It worked and Reddit was on his way. Technology in those days proved not to be as reliable as the working horse!

In the pioneer days of Florida, when "would do, could do or made do" is how it was, settlers learned how to harvest their environment to survive. For medicine, they tapped into the healing properties from plants for cures. One home remedy came from the native scrub prickly pear cactus used for "ground itch" that aggravated the inside of fingers and toes. Reddit says "old families cut the thorns and skin off the cactus then bandaged it over the itch to draw out poison. They also used the aloe plant and honey on burns. One time I was cooking bacon and seared my hand, I used a bar of octagon soap made of hog fat and lye to ease the pain," he adds.

As the talk rambled back to Simmons, he reflects on lessons learned from his parents; the foundation of his life. Simmons was raised by the Golden Rule: "Do unto others as they do unto you." Everyone along the table nodded in unison. "Daddy and mama learned me to take care of myself; not to be a daredevil" (which some of the "cow hunter conclave" say was "insightful"). "My daddy also taught me 'respect.' Today, teens do not have respect for age, you just don't see it." Peggy Cornelius is reminded of a TV documentary she watched about elephant herds, regarding Simmons' thoughts on "respect." She says in elephant herds "old bulls" teach disruptive youths to stay in line in no uncertain terms. "In our human culture, this is not happening, as there are not many strong males or 'old bulls' to teach those lessons."

In earlier times, "traditionally, the term 'Uncle' was used by the family as a term of respect for older family members, as they earned it," adds Al Johnson whose family pioneered in Nokomis near Bradenton, part of Sarasota County. "The term

Al Johnson's Hideaway
Orlando, Florida

'Miss' or 'Mister' was respectfully used to refer to guests." Al Johnson was recently honored by the Florida Cattleman's Association at their annual convention in Marco Island for his long standing contributions to the cattle industry as Honorary Director.

Working cattle all his life, surviving the depression, and long hours of hard work in unpredictable circumstances, Simmons says "was still better than today. We grew our own food, we had kerosene lamps, and didn't have anything, but we had the privilege of improvement; we could make changes. Today, things move too fast and we have less control over our lives. Everything is changing but not for the better. The woods are being bulldozed and people who come here don't know what it used to look like. The population is outnumbering the past. "

Although the "cow hunter" conclave adjourns for another week, the thoughts linger. Everyone climbed aboard their trucks sort of like their horses in the old days with conversation trailing off until the last ones parted. Some of the group left to visit the fort at the Christmas Historical Park and then to lunch for some "finger lickin'" good catfish and cheese grits at the Catfish House in St. Cloud. Although the little roadside restaurant appears to mingle in with other Florida back roads eateries, visitors are greeted here with an amazing surprise. Gracing the walls in every room is a mural of old Florida brought to life with replicas of wild boar, alligators, and wildlife leaping from the canvas landscape.

In days of early settlements after the United States acquired Florida from Spain, land speculators and entrepreneurs came to Florida to seek a fortune in the new territory. By 1825, the year of the first territorial census, there were 5,077 people in all of East Orlando Florida. After the sale of land around Kissimmee to Disneyworld, the small town of Conway became part of Orlando's metropolitan area.

LaGrange (the homestead of Ormond Simmons) was originally a scattered Indian settlement until 1852 when David Nathaniel Carlile arrived from Mississippi with his wife and ten children. The historic Society of North Brevard County restored the 1869 Protestant church that was the center of community gatherings; it is listed on the National Register for Historic Places. According to the Historical Society of North Brevard, LaGrange was located along the primary trade route of the north-south artery of the St. Johns River but to arrive at LaGrange, either men or oxen had to pull their cart of wares two miles from the landing at Salt Lake to reach the community accessible mainly by water.

Population of Titusville (near Ormond Simmons' LaGrange, Florida): 41,712; population of Brevard County – 534,319. Population of Orlando: 799,336; Orange County – 1,043,500; Population of Bradenton (near Nokomis, birth place of Al Johnson): 534,319 – Sarasota County: 36,953.

SEVEN

"THE 1900S DEPRESSION DIDN'T BOTHER COUNTRY PEOPLE BECAUSE WE HAD BETTER SELF-SUFFICIENCY,"

BEEDIE MAE THOMAS, BASINGER, FLORIDA

On the largest remaining tracts of Florida Dry Prairie known as "Seven Mile Slough" in the 1800s and today as Kissimmee Prairie Preserve State Park in Okeechobee was the homestead of the Drayton Redin Kilpatrick family. Twenty-five miles northwest of Okeechobee and another five miles north of County Road 724, the State park was the rangeland of the Kilpatrick family ranch.

The silent beauty of the prairie is more than one hundred miles of sprawling grasslands dotted with yellow, lavender, and pink wildflowers ruffled with flocks of turkeys scurrying beneath spiky palmettos slipping into marshy sloughs. Drayton Kilpatrick must have gazed into the future as far as he could see and envisioned the fruitfulness of this spot as the ideal location to raise his family and his cattle.

Today, this unspoiled prairie is one of most diverse eco-systems in Florida nurturing eighty-six documented butterfly species, the endangered Florida grasshopper sparrow, as well as the crested caracara and sand hill crane. There is 116 miles of multi-use trails for hiking, horseback

The Kilpatrick Homestead
Kissimmee Prairie Preserve State Park
Okeechobee, Florida

riding, and mountain biking that can be traveled without ever seeing another human being. During World War II, the Preserve was used as a B-17 Army

Air Force Bombing Range affirmed by a warning sign posted at the ranger station for visitors to be aware of unexploded ordinances in the park.

Although the original Kilpatrick homestead burned down "my daddy rebuilt the house," says Beedie Mae, Kilpatrick's daughter, and the gate remains open since the last person left, now abandoned behind the park offices at the campground. This is where history began for this family of "cow hunters" who today carry on the tradition in nearby Basinger with Beedie Mae Thomas, 88, and her son R. E. (Ronald Edgar).

Beedie Mae Thomas, daughter of Drayton Redin Kilpatrick and Alice Lanier was born on Prairie Ridge, the old headquarters of the Peavine Railroad, where she grew up with siblings, D.R. (founder of Flaghole in Glades County), Lucille, Charles, Redin, Dillon and Sarah along the dirt road near the Kissimmee River that once linked Fort Drum and Fort Kissimmee, forts constructed during the Seminole Indian Wars. Beedie Mae, born in 1919, according to R.E., is "the oldest living cattle woman in Okeechobee County. She lived the first six years of her life at the Seven Mile Slough homestead and had cattle all her life."

When Beedie Mae was born she was given a "dew lap" heifer calf, a very old tradition initiated by "cow hunters." A young heftier is given as a birthright with its "dew lap" notched as a brand. A "dew lap" is the loose skin underneath the neck or lower jaw of cattle including the "zebu" that has a large dewlap and protruding hump on its underside. In Idaho, the notched "dew lap" is the oldest brand. Tetrads (amphibians), birds, and dogs, such as the English

Springer Spaniel, Bassett Hound, and Mastiff also have large dew laps. For the anole lizard, the dewlap is flared into a bright red flag to intimidate rivals and attract females during mating season. In humans, the dew lap is referred to as a "double chin" and not used to intimidate rivals or attract females.

Drayton Redin Kilpatrick, born at Crabgrass Creek near Orlando, met his wife Alice Lanier when she cooked for railroad workers; she was born at Bull Creek, south of Orlando. The Laniers' date back to pioneer Isaac Lanier who settled near the Kissimmee River and is buried at Cornwell, a former steamboat commerce center in the 1800-1900s, the major form of trade before roads were cut through Florida.

Beedie Mae's daddy, Drayton Redin Kilpatrick, helped construct the old Peavine Railroad that cut through Prairie Ridge where they lived and was a conductor on the Southern Colonization rail that ran from St. Cloud through Kenansville and other 1900s "cow towns." When the railroad pulled out of Kenansville along the Okeechobee spur, Kenansville's livelihood faded but its picturesque memories are still present in the Heartbreak Hotel (now renovated), the bank, and old post office.

Beedie Mae had her parents in her life for only a short time; her mother died in 1932 after her father's death in 1928. It was then that her mother's 300 head of scrub cattle were divided between six children, giving each family member sixty head to start their own ranch. In 1941, after some of the family moved to Jackson County, Beedie's brother, D.R., continued to work in Basinger while Beedie Mae went to school. Beedie Mae dropped out after the eleventh grade because she said she "didn't want to go and board in Okeechobee, as there was no school bus to pick us up in Basinger." However, she stayed in school long enough to meet her future husband Edgar Thomas who lived "around the curve." The Thomas' originally settled in Polk City around 1892. Beedie and Edgar married as teenagers in a Judge's office in Okeechobee; she was sixteen and he was eighteen, the year was 1935.

With horse and plough, the young Thomas' cleared a wooded area for their house in Basinger and with the help of a carpenter "framed doors and windows. The house cost about $300 and we could pay as we went," says Beedie Mae. The Thomas' have five children, Betty Jean was born at home by county Dr. McDermott in 1938, R.E. was born in 1941 at the Sebring Hospital, followed by Alta Lee, Alice, and Debbie.

Living in Basinger meant a long dry spell before modern conveniences. "It wasn't until 1949 that we had electricity, before that we used to pump our

own drinking water and visited the outhouse. Telephones came in 1958," says Beedie Mae. "We were poor as hell but didn't know it," adds R.E. "We didn't need a whole lot. We thought all was fine. Mamma worked in the garden, milked cows, cooked, and when I was 7 or 8 years old, I worked cattle, chopped wood, and fed stock. Mamma made our clothes and quilts from printed feed

sacks. We didn't change clothes a lot or bother to bathe in the washtub but about once a week, heating water on top of the wood-burning stove. We were used to nothing," R.E. explains. "The1900s Depression didn't bother country people because we had better self-sufficiency. We knew how to survive," says Beedie Mae.

As the chief homemaker, Beedie Mae explains how hogs played a major role in their well-being. "We butchered hogs with the help of the children then two or three families divided up the meat. There was no cold storage so we 'rendered out the hog' [used all parts]. We used fat to cook with and stored the lard for about a year in a thirty pound galvanized lard bucket." "Now lard will keep only about thirty days," adds R.E. "We also made sausage and smoked bacon. We used the intestines for sausage casings and smoked ham in the smokehouse," explains Beedie Mae. She says a "small hog could give you two or three meals. Without refrigeration, we used two blocks of ice and kept meat in a burlap bag. The ice lasted three or four days so we could also make iced tea." For other supplies and staples, the community patronized the Henry Sloan Country Store that long ago deteriorated.

The women were the glue of the family. Beedie Mae says she "got up at sunrise and milked the cows before making a breakfast of eggs or oatmeal with clabber (soured cured milk), biscuits, and cornbread. Everyone in the family started each day with breakfast together before splitting up the daily chores. We raised corn, peas, sweet potatoes, green turnips, peas, beans, and collards in the garden then jarred them up for next year," explains Beedie Mae. "The men were out cow hunting for about two weeks on a crew and we had no contact. I had to manage the children and the homestead during long, unknown periods of time and through all crises."

In order to survive independently, early settlers divided their labor into various tasks. The daily working of cattle, however, was not exclusively the chore of men. Beedie Mae remembers when she worked in the pens, at the parting gates (shoots), and raised little dairy calves which extended into R.E.'s current business of raising replacement heifers. "When I milked the cows," says Beddie Mae, "I used a long pole with a loop on the end to put around the cow's horns to keep her still; Brahman cows gave no cream or 'blue john'." [The provincial dictionary defines "blue john" as a term for "skim milk.]. Although Beedie Mae says she didn't ride a horse much then, she calls herself a "jeep cowgirl."

As a little community, "we passed time with swamp cabbage cook-outs and fish fries, gator, and frog hunting, and once a week we ate a big family meal saving leftovers for the rest of the week. Families were important then and depended on each other. People didn't travel, so you might not see anyone for a week," Beedie Mae says.

The people of Basinger, like R.E., reflect an independent spirit reminiscent of their heritage as pioneer "cow hunters." R.E. has no cell phone, no computer, and no credit cards. His principle is that if you "live simple, you can live better." He says he is a "die hard, still today. R.E. built "Tater Ridge" across the road from his ranch and near Beedie Mae's. "Tater Ridge is an open air structure with rusted, old ranch tools hanging from the walls, a wood burning stove in the corner, and a large wooden table and benches stretching the length of the dirt floor. This is where the family gathers to shell peas or enjoy a finger-lickin' good barbecue without worrying about all the drippings.

R.E. and his wife Judy, raise replacement heifers for dairies. R.E. says the life span of a dairy cow is 6 or 7 years with beef cattle living longer, 10 to 12 years. R.E.

R.E.'s "Pea Palace" at Tater Ridge.

describes their ranch as "a small four hundred and fifty acre place but the land value is ten times higher than what a cow can generate for one acre; however, I won't get rid of anything. There is a philosophy of a cattle rancher: The first generation makes it; the second generation keeps it; the third generation spends it." As Beedie Mae says, "You have to want to do ranching. If you don't have a love of the land, you can't make a living or support a family. You can't buy land now and start a ranch. You can try, but I don't see how you can do it. It comes down to economics. The bigger ranches, however, will survive."

One aspect of the cattle business that R.E. and Beedie Mae stress is that the consumer today demands a higher quality of beef. "Cattle are healthier if they are grass fed but instead of selling a cow at five hundred pounds, to get its weight up to a thousand pounds on grass, you lose profit," according to R.E., thus, Florida cattle are sold at the market and sent to feedlots to gain additional weight before slaughter. R. E. and Judy have two sons, Randy, an Okeechobee Deputy Sheriff, and Danny, a school teacher, soon-to-be college professor.

There is no turning back the clock to the days when "cattle roamed free range in Florida and no one paid for anything," says R.E. "Cattle grazed on tall grasses of the rolling prairie until the 1940's when fence laws were passed. People bought land and fenced it in. Before, cattle used to run together and were sorted out when they went to market. In the early days, there were no improvements; it was all woods, now we have improved pasture. In 1948, we cleared the pasture with tractors and burned woods for more fertile land. In today's modern age of urbanized agriculture, you don't have to do much labor, then it was a lot of work but you got all the profit from the cows. Selling twenty cows at $7.00 a head, you could buy four or five acres of land. Now it takes twenty cows to buy one acre. We bought the first eighty acres from a tax deed costing $25.00."

Living in the isolated wilds of old Florida meant families were tight and neighbors pulled together during unexpected natural disasters. During the furious 1928 hurricane that ripped across the heart of Lake Okeechobee inland, a razor sharp piece of tin sheered off the roof of the Fitzpatrick's house as Drayton and Alice rushed to gather up all the kids, bracing against roaring winds and rain, to evacuate several miles to the nearest neighbor.

Besides the threat of unannounced hurricanes, there was an imminent threat of fire. "Once there was a close call when a fire almost burned up our house," recalls Beedie Mae. "Mr. Jim Durance was burning off woods when a roaring fire approached within fifty yards of our front door before it finally burned out. At least the fire didn't destroy the lemon tree planted in front of the house by Christine Durance over a hundred years ago," Beedie Mae says relieved, as she points to it from across the wooden porch where a gentle breeze flutters its leaves on long sturdy branches reaching toward the sky.

Through the early 1900s, the forty-three mile Kissimmee River, meandering alongside Basinger, was the main source of commercial enterprise until cars became the expedient mode of transportation. Soon state roads were carved through the lone prairie and graceful paddle boats that plied the river from 1894 through the 1920's delivering passengers, horses, mail, and other wares to the small settlements gradually disappeared as the river trade died.

Okeechobee, the stepchild of Basinger, further developed as a "cow town" when the railroad by-passed Basinger and a depot was built there. Although Basinger never grew into a major economic center, it had its heyday as a bustling cattle community with two hotels, a general store, post office, and churches. In the 1870s, early settlers in Basinger were the Holmes, Raulersons, Chandlers, and Underhills on the Okeechobee County side and the Pearces and Daughtrys in Highlands County across the River. The 1800's homestead of Edna Pearce Lockett, the granddaughter of John Mizell Pearce that overlooks the Kissimmee River at Fort Basinger in Highlands County, remains protected. Lockett was the teacher at the one room school house now located on her estate. "The actual Fort Basinger was originally built further west," R.E. points out.

Edna Pearce Lockett's granddaddy, Captain John Mizell Pearce was born in 1834, and served in the Third Seminole War, 1855-58 and Civil War as a Captain. He established a large cattle business originally headquartered in Fort Meade until he moved to Fort Basinger 1875. He built a house and set up a ferryboat operation along the river with his steamboat *Mary Belle*. Rates on the *Mary Belle* were reasonable: Man and horse, 25 cents; horse and buggy, 50 cents; a yoke of oxen and cart, 40 cents. Capt. Pearce died in 1897 at Fort Basinger and his widow built the home where Mrs. Edna Pearce Lockett lived. William Sidney Pearce, Captain Pearce's son, built the first bridge across the Kissimmee River in 1916, connecting the two different county Basingers'.

"Then in 1960, the Kissimmee River began to be channeled by the Army Corp of Engineers to drain the land. Locks were put in up in Lake Okeechobee," explains R.E. "Orlando was drained through Kissimmee about the time that Disneyland was in the planning stages as they needed water. Here in Basinger, we had one extreme or another; sometimes there was no water under the house, to a lot of water. Now water doesn't stay all day in the ditches." The Kissimmee River Restoration project continues today on 40 square miles of river/floodplain ecosystems and 26,500 acres of wetlands. The project is designated "to revive native habitat, establish a reliable supply of water for Florida, and flood control consistent with restoration. The state invested more than $2 billion to preserve the Everglades and $140 million to improve the health of Lake Okeechobee," (wwww.dep.state.fl.us/evergladesforever).

Basinger today thrives in unspoiled beauty along this remote section of U.S. 98 with only the Cracker Trail Country store and gas station as a stop-over between Lorida and Okeechobee. It is one place on the Kissimmee prairie where eagles soar, birds sing, butterflies flit silently across fields of wildflowers, and cows contentedly chew their cud in the cool shadow of thickly woven trees. The original family descendants, whose ancestors settled the land, still maintain the homesteads within the seven mile range of Basinger. According to the Okeechobee County Clerk's office, the population of Basinger is based on an estimated 400 voters within the precinct.

EIGHT

"I AM A TRUE 'FLORIDA CRACKER' BUT WITH A LITTLE EXTRA SALT!"

IRIS WALL: INDIANTOWN PIONEER "COW HUNTRESS"

Whether it is hunting "piney wood rooters," parting cows, rounding up wild horses, hunting alligators or heading-up the six family owned W&W Lumber Yards, Iris Wall is at home in what she says "is the best town on Earth" Indiantown, Florida.

Looking across the pasture not far from her modest residence is Iris' herd of thirty DNA tested and registered "Cracker Cows" who make a rowdy, bellowing entrance when Iris calls them for an extra treat of grain. There are several small herds of cracker cattle scattered across the state in an attempt to preserve them. These cracker cattle date back to the arrival of the Spanish Conquistadors near St. Augustine in the 1500s. After the Spanish left, "they turned loose cows, hogs, and cattle that the new settlers hunted down. You couldn't just go and lasso some cows roaming in open prairie; you had to hunt them out of hard to get places, the swamps, woods, and thick palmettos. This is how they got their name: 'cow hunters.' The early pioneers of the 1800s gathered the horses and cows and sold them to the Confederacy and the Union. The 'cracker cattle' are tough; they are adapted to Florida's climate and are able to live on nothing." Iris Wall is a long-time member and Vice President of the Florida Cracker Cattle Association.

Following her intention to "support the best of Florida" Iris Wall also is a member of the Florida Cracker Trail Association, a non-profit organization that supports the preservation of the old cracker trail from Bradenton to Fort Pierce; the old trail that "cow hunters" used to herd thousands of cattle to market from coast-to-coast.

Iris is also on the Board of Directors of the Cracker Horse Association. She says, "people like 'cracker horses' because they aren't affected by the heat, they run like a steak of lightning, have a calm nature, and are easy keepers." Riding her own cracker horse, "Abraham," Iris has participated in the Great Cracker Trail Ride of 1995, celebrating Florida's 150 years of statehood and the "Great Florida Cattle Drive of Ought 6" that got underway in Osceola County and ended in Kenansville. Standing firmly on her belief to "keep old Florida alive," she says "agriculture is disappearing."

Born in 1929 as a fifth generation Floridian and Native daughter of Indiantown, Iris' was born to Lois Roland and Cecil Pollock. Her grandparents, Anna and Alonza Roland moved to the little community from Chancy Bay near Canal Point.

At 77, Iris Wall is still a working "cow girl," or what she prefers to be called a "cow hunter," "It's what I have been doing all my life. When I was just a little girl in the 1940s, I remember the screwworm epidemic. I used to ride with some benzene in my saddle pockets. I would squirt it in the cow's naval to get the worms to work their way to the surface. Then you had to take some palmettos or anything to scrape them out. There were hundreds of maggots that hatched from flies. After you got out the screwworms, you painted the wound with a tar-like substance called 'Smear-X.' Anytime there was fresh blood on an animal, the fly would lay its eggs and they would hatch into worms. In the early 50's, the University of Florida sent out a bulletin saying that they were going to turn loose millions of sterile flies from an airplane. Many old 'crackers' laughed, but it worked."

From her earliest memories, Iris learned to nurture and work the land and helped her daddy gather up and part cows/calves during the calving season. We drove more than 100 head of daddy's cattle from Indiantown to Palm City. We would get up before the cows 'got out off the bed.' After the calves nurse, the 'baby sitter cows' take the calves away so the mother can feed. At a certain time, the cows walk to water, then they go to rest and lie down."

"As a young teen, I worked cattle alongside 'cow hunters' who trusted me like a Queen. My dad worked for Mr. Williamson during my early teens and I would ride thirteen miles out to their ranch and be there by daylight to go cow hunting. However, there is one story that Mr. J. C. Bass tells on me when I was parting cattle. There were a bunch of cows in a crevasse when one of them broke out and I got thrown on my back. Daddy just rode over, looked down at me said, 'Gal, you can do better than that!'"

"Sometimes we would gather cattle weeks at a time and with no fences, the gathering was much different from today. After we gathered about 100 head, the children would hold the cattle while the men rode  out to the sides and gathered more cattle and drove them to the herd. When we heard the whips and dogs ahead of us we knew to speed up, but when they were behind us, we stopped and waited. We had a man that would lead out 'on point' and we had an old black cow that we called 'old lead cow' that would follow the point man and lead the herd. My dad always said, "If you learn to think like a cow you don't need a rope, and you never let a cow take a step except in the direction you want him to go."

"Daddy would go to Carry's Cattle Auction in Tampa and buy every old horse to give us kids and he would say, 'Go to it!' That is exactly what we did. I learned how to 'gentle-down' a horse, so I guess I was the first 'horse whisperer.'"

It was about the sixth grade that the self-described "strong willed redhead" met her lifelong partner, Homer, who was born in Montana and moved to Indiantown when he was a toddler. However, when Homer and Iris began courting at Martin County High School, "charming" her, she said "wasn't all easy going," even though, unbeknownst to him, "I had my eye on Homer since the first time I saw him." Perhaps it was the sixth grade play, *Aunt Drusilla's Garden* that turned the glimmer in his eye into romance when Iris starred as Aunt Drusilla and Homer, the Gardner. "We used to fuss and fight" but near the end of high school Homer somehow got up the courage to gingerly ask Iris, in his own special way, for a date: "Do you think you might be able to get a dress for the prom?" In her usual manner, Iris had already made up her mind and the rest led to their marriage in 1948 after high school, graduating in a class of 38 students. They were eighteen years old and "we spent the next forty-seven years in a marvelous life. "We cow hunted together with two hound dogs, rode the woods, hunted, and fished. It was wonderful."

The young couple also had their adventurous close calls. "On the night Terry was born, we were on the way to the hospital at West Palm Beach and Homer was driving after he had gotten bit on his finger by a hog. I told the doctors to take care of Homer and the baby. Hogs have a very infectious bite." Then there was the time when Iris was threatened by the largest specie of Florida snake, the Diamondback rattler. Iris and Homer were feeding horses under some cabbage palms where there were a lot of dead leaves. "I heard the dogs yelping then I heard the rattle. Homer shouted, 'Don't move!' The rattler was moving under the palmettos. Homer pushed me hard, hit the snake on the head with a big stick, and killed it. It was a huge!" Iris was also confronted by some daring moccasins that caught her off guard. "I was pulling along a corn sack behind some others who were gigging frogs and putting them in the bag. I suddenly had an eerie feeling as I walked along so I looked behind me. There were two big moccasins following me and the sack. I hit the bank and left the sack."

"In 1994, as a last effort to fight Homer's cancer, I took him to a clinic in Mexico but it was futile. In his last words he said, 'Don't feel sorry, Iris, we had all this time to tell each other how much we loved one another. This is not the end. What we'll have in Heaven will be better than what we had here on Earth.'"

Today, Iris Wall manages a sprawling 1,200 acre ranch where she not only works cows, monitors the water levels, and pastures but retreats into the woods from the creeping urbanization along the fringes. Referring to herself as a "woods rat," it is amidst the tall pines, oaks, and scrub that Iris replenishes her mind, body, and spirit strengthening her strong faith in God. As one of the founders of the Family Worship Center in Indiantown, she is a Sunday school teacher for adult women "whom I have known for more than fifty years." One of Iris' three daughters, Eva Edwards, says her mother is the "family glue and epitome of a 'cracker,' she never gives up. With her love of Nature, mother is an example of appreciating what God put on Earth." All three daughters Terry Gilliam, Jonnie Flewelling, Eva Edwards and their husbands, who manage the W&W Lumber Yards, work in the family business. Iris and Homer started the lumber business in 1962 with a partner whom they bought out three years later. Homer sold lumber around Lake Okeechobee and Iris ran the lumber yard with baby Eva slung on her hip. "We started with nothing and eventually bought the business." Today, there are six regional W&W Lumber Yards in Florida.

Besides her business accomplishments, Iris says she is most proud of our children and grandchildren. One granddaughter, Whitney, a hair stylist, maintains Iris' well-coiffed appearance whether she is getting ready for the trail or preparing to give one of her many talks. But, despite the demure appearance of her brood, Iris says their "kids were raised to shoot an alligator in the eye, hunt wild hogs, and appreciate Nature."

Iris Wall's life is inseparable from the land. "Everyday I ride the pastures not just to work, I come here to rest." Along an almost hidden path off a rutted road, Iris says "this is one of my favorite spots." Climbing over a couple of fallen trees nestled into native brush, she steps onto a small rise and pauses "to listen" to utter silence; the only lingering sounds are the trill of birds and little critters rustling beneath the leaves. "This is old Florida and this is what I want to preserve. At one time in Florida, the water was so pure you could drink from a gator hole. But, today, the habitat is threatened by development everywhere in Florida. In the last fifteen years,

I've seen only two Florida Panthers. It was one time when Judge Bailey, his wife, Carol and I were riding on the grade at the ranch in a cool, rainy mist and I said, 'There's a cat!' Carole said, 'I think it's a Florida panther!"

Bumping along in Iris's pick-up truck is like riding with a "cow girl" parting cattle over pastures, underneath trees, weaving in and out of languid cows and calves lulling in the cool afternoon breeze as the road intertwines up to a picturesque wooden cabin perhaps inclined to greet a couple of bone-tired "cow hunters" dusting off their boots to take a respite on the porch after a long trail ride. But, for now, the cabin is quiet until a young brood of grandchildren or school kids stop by to visit with Iris and hear her own stories about her unique experiences carving a life from the wilds of Indiantown. Based on her belief in educating youth about Nature and Florida's native habitat, Iris addresses many young people. "I never turn down an invitation to speak to children. Recently, I brought a buckboard full of second graders from Warfield Elementary school here and took them on a tour. I showed them the cow pens, explained the brand on the cattle's shoulders, and showed them the difference between a slough and marsh. We were raised on cowboy and Indian movies, but the cartoons children watch today are very unhealthy. One of the kids came inside the cabin and asked me if it was OK to jump up and down on the bunk beds, I said 'sure.' I want them to experience life in the country and have an understanding of agriculture. I love children."

"However, I didn't come out here to this cabin for sometime after Homer passed away in 1994 but I finally decided I must go on with my life and began to fix the place up. I bring the children here to enjoy the way people used to live in early Florida." Perched above an open pasture and a backdrop of tall oaks, the peacefulness of the cabin in the rustic setting inspires freedom. "One night my teenage grandson and I stayed up all night right here just talking. Isn't that something that a grandmother can have this kind of relationship with a grandson with all these years in between us?"

But for years, the ranch with its entire family heritage, remained without a name until one day "my daughter Jonnie and I were headed from the house to the ranch when she turned to me and said, 'Mom, I'm tired of telling people to just cross the railroad tracks, go two miles west of town on State Road 710, and make a right into the ranch. You need to give the ranch a name.'" As is her way, a woman of action with little hesitation, Iris recaptured the words of her beloved late husband, Homer: "The worst position a person can be in is when they have to climb off their high horse." These words stuck and the ranch now welcomes visitors through wooden portals with the proud words "High Horse Ranch."

The early Lower Creek Indians from Georgia were already settled at Indiantown when Iris' grandparents discovered the rustic beauty of "real Florida," a moniker for the community today. The Lower Creek Indians migrated into Florida to escape the dominance of the Upper Creeks. The high elevation, 35 feet above sea level, was an ideal site to support their livelihood of fishing, hunting, and agriculture. Along with other Southern tribes, the Indians became known as "Seminoles" derived from the word "Myskoke" of the Creek language and "simano-li," an adaptation of the Spanish word "Cimarron" which meant to Europeans: "Wild" or "wild men."

By the 1900s and Florida's "boom days," the little settlement began to attract the attention of northern entrepreneurs with its ideal location 30 miles inland from the east coast and 30 miles southeast of the second largest fresh water lake in the United States. Lake Okeechobee. One of these visionaries, who recognized the opportunity for growth in Indiantown with the U.S. Army Corp of Engineers construction of the cross-state canal, was S. Davies Warfield, a Baltimore financier and railroad tycoon who wanted to expand the rails from Central Florida to West Palm Beach.

Solomon Davies Warfield was born in Maryland in 1859. During the 1880s, he established and built a Baltimore company to manufacture his invention of corn cutters (a small utensil to peel corn) and silkers. In 1898, he was associated with John Skelton Williams and started the Seaboard Air Line Railway Company in 1900. Warfield was also President of Old Bay Line, a passenger vessel on the Chesapeake Bay. In honor of Warfield, a steamer was christened: The S.S. President Warfield. In the 40s, the vessel carried trans-Atlantic passengers to the United Kingdom and later became part of the U.S. Navy. The vessel was involved in stowing immigrants into Palestine and was finally moored in Israel. Leon Uris used the vessel in his novel, Exodus, but it later burned to the waterline and was scrapped.

However, after visiting Florida, Warfield's dream focused on Indiantown where he envisioned a resort community and central southern headquarters for his Seaboard Airline Railroad (or Seaboard Coastline), as well as the seat of Martin County (formed in 1925); thus, he began to buy up large parcels of land. Warfield masterminded a model city, laid out streets, built a school and houses, and the majestic Seminole Inn. With grand flair and drama, Warfield opened the Inn in 1927 with a celebrated guest list including his niece, Wallace Simpson, who became the Duchess of Windsor when she married the King of England. Edward abdicated the throne to marry the divorcee. The legacy of Wallace Simpson's famous words lasted longer than her royalty: "You can never be too thin, or too rich."

Warfield's dream of the wilderness resort town never came to fruition during his lifetime when he died the same year the Inn opened. With the Great Depression lurking across the country, the ornate 19th-20th Century Revival structure remained silent along State Road 710 for another decade with little success to revive it by a new consortium of investors who took hold of Warfield's interests as the "Indian Town Development Company" until 1953 when it was renamed "Indiantown Company, Inc." However, according to Iris, not known to many, "Indiantown" was formerly known as "Annie" after the revered Mrs. Annie Platt. The Platt's were old time Florida pioneers.

In 1970, Homer and Iris bought the Seminole Inn and renovated it. Today, Iris' daughter, Jonnie Flewelling manages the Inn, listed on the National Registry of Historic Places. The Seminole Inn provides visitors from all over the world a trip back in time through its historic charm and ambiance. There's nothing like enjoying fried chicken and all the fixin's, fried green tomatoes, and Southern green beans in the stately Windsor Dining room where royalty were once served. Iris said they bought and restored the Inn "as a gift to the town." Part of Iris Wall's mission today is to "encourage small owners to practice good stewardship with the increasing urbanization of Florida."

With all that Iris has accomplished in her lifetime, she still has more to do. Iris Wall believes in "stewardship" and most importantly her children but her growing concern is with the overdevelopment and urbanization of Florida. "Developers want the land. I will never sell one inch of it. They aren't making any more land and the government is not making it easy to hold onto. There is so much corruption in politics and money is so important. The politicians are unconcerned about a way of life. When Homer and I had no money, it was a small factor in our life."

"Today, real estate is out-of-site. People are building castles to live in. I tell some of the senior seniors I talk to that they live in a climate controlled environment. They have no knowledge of the weather. But I say when you start to see dust on your boots, you better think about saving water. These planned communities are providing an unrealistic way of life. Does every small community need a ball park, an equestrian center, and expensive playgrounds? The whole nation needs to come off the 'high horse.'"

"Developers are always interested in buying our land but I don't want to sell one acre as it would mean more money to developers and less agriculture; the agriculture industry is going down the drain."

"In the beef industry, Florida is the twelfth producer in the nation in 2006-07 but ranchers are being forced to sell in order to pay unrealistic tax bills or inheritance taxes. In order for ranchers to keep their property, they need to get a tax break and not be told by the government what to do. Ranchers have always taken care of the land. Today, most ranchers are land rich and dollar poor. It's a hard life. My grandpa had a big garden and grew food; he had chickens and cows. But, I don't know what to do if conviction to save agriculture isn't deeper."

"Life is not a pot of gold at the end of a rainbow, or success. Life is being satisfied every day. Life is having trust in people. Today, there is a conception of success that equals money, but the best and miserable have had money and fame, it does not bring happiness. I was born dirt poor but I know I've done my best and I have a happy life. I have the best friends all over the state and a family I love."

Iris Wall's optimism echoes through the whispering pines, the land, and is implicit in her genuine smile and determined nature. She is living proof of her philosophy: "Be whatever you want to be and keep you word."

Acting on her convictions, Iris Wall is on the Board of the Martin County Farm Bureau and member of the Florida and National Cattlemen's Association. Next to the Indiantown Library in Kiwanis Park is the "Homer Wall Gazebo"

1900's
Homer and Iris Wall

constructed from the trust funds of the U.S. Generating Company. Homer Wall was a founding member of the Indiantown Kiwanis Club and devoted his life to the community. Iris Wall was selected as the "Woman of the Year in Agriculture 2006" by Florida Agriculture Commissioner Charles H. Bronson.

Located on the Treasure Coast Indiantown is in unincorporated Martin County that has a history of exploration when in the 1700s, Spanish galleons carrying cargos of gold and silver were wrecked in hurricanes along the coast. Pioneers arrived by boat and land, planted pineapples, citrus, and raised cattle. By 1894, Henry Flagler constructed the Florida East Coast Railway from Jacksonville to Miami expanding the economy into tourism.

Martin County was named for John W. Martin, Governor of Florida from 1925 to 1929; the county seat is Stuart. According to the 2000 U.S. Census, Martin County had a population of 126,731, estimated to be 139,728 in 2005, a 10% percent increase over five years compared to the State growth at 11.3% for the same period.

The population of unincorporated Indiantown in the 2000 census: 5,588. Indiantown is also the home of Payson Park, one of the top Thoroughbred horse racing facilities in the United States.

NINE

A GATEWAY OF GOODWILL TO THE WORLD

FLORIDA CATTLEMEN: BUD ADAMS, PARKE WRIGHT AND JIM STRICKLAND
CUBA

It's quite a surprise to see the Premier of the Republic of Macedonia wearing a Stetson, and perhaps even more of a surprise to learn that Florida cattle ranchers are working on exporting live animals to the southernmost part of the former Socialists Federation of Yugoslavia, but this is the cultural and economic bridge being extended around the world by two Florida cattlemen: Bud Adams and Jim Strickland.

Build a bridge; change the world, if there is a beginning point in establishing human relations with countries that bare economic fruition, it is by lending a hand to populations that are deficient in protein due to their geographic location, political turmoil, and difficulty in moving from a socialist to a capitalist economy. An initiative in this direction was pursued by Adams (The Adams Ranch, Ft. Pierce, Strickland Ranch, Myakka) and Parke Wright in 2003 when Wright negotiated a shipment of cattle to Cuba. Although the 1962 trade embargo remains in effect by the U.S., in October 2003 Adams, Strickland, and Wright traveled to Cuba under a seal obtained from the U.S. Department Treasury to do business there under legislation signed into law by President Bill Clinton in 2000 that permits direct sale of agricultural and humanitarian products to the country. Today, many U.S. corporations such as Cargill and Monsanto are shipping grain and seed products into Cuba through the permission of Pedro Alvarez, Director of Cuba's government owned Alimport Company. Cargill, which has been doing business with Cuba since 2000 in the amount of 300,000 tons of a wide variety of food products, recently signed a $4 million contract to sell wheat and soy protein to the island.

In a *Florida Trend Magazine* article, Tim Lynch, Director Emeritus of the Center for Economic Forecasting and Analysis at Florida State University, said prior to 1959, Florida was Cuba's largest state trading partner with only a "trickle" of agriculture being sent today. He forecasts that with a normalization of trade between Cuba and the U.S., it could result in a $1.3 billion to $2.5 billion growth in the Florida GDP over the next 30 years.

The 2003 cattle shipment to Cuba was scheduled to include 80 Brangus from Strickland's ranch, 80 Brafords from the Adams Ranch and 80 Beef Masters. The heifers, with three bulls from each breed, comprised the Florida shipment valued at half million dollars. However, before the cattle could leave from Port Manatee in March for Port Mariel in Cuba, a Washington state cow slaughtered in December was diagnosed with "mad cow" disease or Bovine Spongiform Encephalopathy (BSE). The affected dairy cow originated in Canada that allegedly allowed animal parts to be added to cattle feed. Thus, Cuba and a number of other countries banned the import of U.S. beef and the deal was postponed.

"The U.S. Department of Agriculture prohibits the addition of animal parts to feed," Adams added. Wright, whose family began shipping cattle to Cuba in 1850 (Lykes Brothers) had previously arranged the sale of 150 Vermont and New York dairy cows to Cuba in a similar transaction.

When the trio visited the island, they were escorted to the western pastures by host Ramon Castro, elder brother of Fidel. Adams said the tour was an "eye opener as the Cuban people had consumed most of the cattle and they needed beef and milk to feed the people. After the Soviets departed from Cuba leaving behind many unfulfilled promises, Ramon Castro said the Soviets were supposed to leave fuel and fertilizer to gear the island's agriculture towards growing feed for chickens and hogs. When Russia pulled out, crops couldn't grow resulting in the people being denied protein with an unbalanced diet of beans, rice, and sugar. There isn't enough protein and meat in Cuba for young people at a developing age," Adams added. "When

Fidel came into power, Cuba had a progressive cattle industry but Castro said that everyone could eat beef. Prior to Castro, beef was reserved only for the rich. So they slaughtered the entire cow herd and then there was no beef. But, Cuba has great grass and a good climate similar to Florida; our cattle can easily adapt. Although the Soviets left no tractors, cows can till the soil eating grass. Seed stock herds provide bulls for breeding to build a commercial herd for slaughter. The Soviets also did not come through in price support for sugar, so good grass is available from former sugar land. Cuba has good cattlemen and veterinarians; the problem they face is how to do things. They are interested in the American way of raising cattle," Adams explained.

Adams and Strickland were the first American ranchers to go to Cuba since the embargo to help negotiate beef sales. After Cuba lifted its ban on the importation of U.S. beef, Pedro Alvarez sent a letter to Jim Strickland as the first country to accept live cattle from the U.S. Adams was approached again by the Cuban government to send a shipment of cattle. "By this time, the eight month old heifer calves were fourteen months. If they wanted another crop they would have to wait until the next year," said Adams. These negotiations continued every year but he never received a contract for delivery. "It's easy for me every day to sell cattle in the U.S. For example, I recently shipped some ten year olds to Texas for $1,100, it not hard to sell our cattle, but it is a pain to deal with Cuba."

Several years later, Adams did join in with Strickland through Wright in selling a small number of cattle to Cuba. "Anytime there is a transaction, it's a good deal. Cuba is only 90 miles away from a good market and they need cattle," Adams added. Cuba today buys "shipments of dairy cows from Canada," said Strickland.

Importing cattle to Cuba involves lengthy contracts, health protocols,

clearances, quarantines, shipping regulations, and people to make financial arrangements. "Cuba deals in 'cash only' transactions as part of the U.S. requirement that Cuba not be extended any credit; it is a complicated process as money has to go through many channels before the ship leaves the dock with cattle aboard for Port Mariel. It is the hardest country to deal with," Strickland said. "When a cowman sells a cow today, he expects to get paid today," Adams emphasized. "Even though it is easier to sell cattle in the United States, exporting cattle is subject to change.

In a good year, when there is a surplus of cattle in the U.S., new markets are good."

One caveat to exporting cattle to Cuba is "bluetongue," a viral infection from a gnat that occurs in southern Florida and the Western Hemisphere. It doesn't dramatically affect the health of cattle but is tested for on imports to Cuba due to its transmutability to sheep, one of the largest herds in Cuba. "A University of Florida virologist said that even if a cow tests positive for bluetongue, there is no danger of the strain affecting the herd," Strickland said. According to the National Library of Medicine, serological surveys of cattle, sheep, and goats confirm that bluetongue virus (BTV) is common in Florida, Puerto Rico and St. Croix in the U.S. and in other Caribbean countries including Guyana and Suriname in South America. Bluetongue is a dormant disease present with different strains and has been present since the 1940's in Florida cattle.

In terms of other world markets, "there is a strong demand for boxed or live beef and by-products such as hides and tripe," Strickland said. "There is an export market open for live cattle that does help to change the price structure of cattle in the United States."

In June of 2007, Swift and Company was purchased by J&F Particpacoes S.A. of Brazil, the largest beef processor in that country for $225 million, assuming $1.2 billion in debt, according to an article by Troy Marshall in *Beef Magazine* that provides the company with access to the two largest beef markets in the world: The United States and Asia with potential sales of nearly $12 billion and an increase in its beef-processing capacity; Brazilian beef is currently banned from Asia. "There is a demand for beef in Romania and other countries and presently we are working on a bid for cattle exports to Honduras. On July 18, 2007, we sent the first American shipment of pure bred Brahman heifers and bulls off of Duck Smith's son, Dan Smith's, Wauchula Crescent Bar D ranch to Guyana, as well as the first pure bred Brangus cattle from Little Creek Farm in Alachua," said Strickland. He is also flying to Guyana at the end of August 2007 with a forage specialist from the University of Florida to sign a reciprocal agreement with the University in Guyana for exchange of information to help them with the Guyana ranch project. Other markets Renee and Jim Strickland are pursuing are Costa Rica, Panama, Honduras, Macedonia and potentially Moscow," said Strickland.

In the foreign markets, including Cuba, Adams said that "composite" cattle are more functional as they are "a hybrid cow that has increased production up to 25%. In composite cows, one breed compliments the other with more efficient conformation. An open-ended program brings in various types of bulls with selection to improve the herd," Adams explained. Always looking to expand the Florida cattle market, Adams is also experimenting with a new Hemarthria grass that can grow year round. The Florida variety of Hemarthia is providing year round growth in South Florida.

"The price of exports all over the world is set by supply and demand. The more markets the stronger the demand," explained Strickland, "Florida beef is the best in the world. We do not have hoof-and-mouth as other beef producing countries that are not eligible to go into Cuba. But a lot of countries are working to clean up cattle diseases."

Florida cattlemen enjoying the shade of a veranda
Cuba

"We have a good export market now in Central and South America," stated Strickland. "Florida cattlemen are in a position to help those countries with live animals. To further the ability for exports to be shipped to international destinations, we are working to build a permanent quarantine facility in Indiantown; it's now a temporary station. Presently, exports are permitted by the United States Department of Agriculture to ship cattle on a case-by-case basis," he added.

"The cost to renovate the current quarantine facility is approximately $135,000, as it needs concrete and a roof. We can use prison labor to cut costs. It is a facility where international buyers can visit and see cattle displayed. Bud Adams has displayed his bulls there. The facility can hold 150-175 cattle. Charles Bronson, Florida's Commissioner of Agriculture and Doyle Conner of the Florida Agriculture Department, endorse the idea of displaying cattle to potential buyers. The permanent facility status requires USDA sanction," said Strickland.

Strickland believes that Japan, famous for their very expensive "massaged" Kobe beef, "tried to keep U.S. beef banned from import there and used 'mad cow' disease as an excuse to keep their market closed. 'Mad cow' is not contagious and results from adding animals parts to cattle feed that is prohibited in the United States. Today, there are no export limits on cattle to other countries by the State Department, Treasury, or Department of Agriculture." Adams said in U.S. beef market, "we have to compete with imports, but we are efficient enough to compete successfully. We should have a country of origin label law that allows consumers to know if their beef comes from outside the U.S. Our present law is unworkable."

Bud Adams feeding fish Cross 7 Ranch, Ft.Pierce

The potential of the Florida cattle industry, both internationally and nationally, is on the precipice of expansion. Both Bud Adams and Jim Strickland are investigating "natural beef" production. Adams said "there may be a market for natural beef. Our cattle are raised on pasture without antibiotics or implants. We would have to find a feeder that would pay for these cattle." Strickland added that "there is economic potential in producing 'natural' beef, requiring a feedlot that does not use hormones."

Both Bud Adams and Jim Strickland are pioneer cattle ranchers. Adams joined the ranch after graduating from University of Florida in 1948 when Alto Adams, Sr., a Florida Supreme Court Judge bought land in Ft. Pierce, west of town, in 1937 "that no one wanted." Bud Adams started crossing Hereford and Brahman cattle in 1948 when the original crosses occurred. After twenty years, by 1970, Brafords were designated by the USDA as the first Adams Braford Foundation Herd. Today, Bud Adams' sons and grandchildren manage and operate the Crossed–Seven Ranch where he and his wife, Dot, live in a modest ranch-style home surrounded by fruit trees they planted 59 years ago.

Strickland and his wife Renee own "Strickland Exports" in Myakka and a new company "Strickland Ranch and Exports." Besides raising cattle, they ship hogs, sheep, goats, and other live animals to markets around the world. Strickland's granddaddy, Andrew Jackson Strickland moved from Georgia to Florida in the 1800s; Jim Strickland is a fourth generation cattle rancher, second Vice President of the Florida Cattleman's Association, and agricultural property appraiser in Manatee County.

TEN

A LIVING HERITAGE: THE OLD WAYS, THE MEDICINES, AND TECHNOLOGY

Don Mara and Rodney Miner
Preserving Florida History

Wearing the authentic working clothes of an 1800's "cow hunter" at the "Kowtown Festival" in Kissimmee, historians Don Cox and Rodney Miner, cast light upon the rugged lifestyle of Florida's legendary pioneers. When New World explorers in the 1500s were sent from Europe to conquer lands across the Atlantic, the fertile rich plains of the peninsula were enticing for the expansion of European empires. For more than two centuries, Florida territories flew under five different international flags including the Spanish, English, and French.

The earliest recorded maps of the peninsula according to Cox's research of the Florida Historical Quarterly, indicates that before Ponce de Leon arrived, "there were other sailors, John Cabot, 1497, who already knew of the peninsula, recognized by geographical features that picture a large island designated as "Zeponu insula," or Japan with references to the Gulf of Mexico, an extremity in the direction of the Florida peninsula. In Peter Martyr's ship maps,"Legatio Babyloncia Occeani Decas of 1511," north of Cuba there is a land area named "Isla de Beimeni Parte" believed to be recorded before Ponce de Leon's expedition in the 1500s."

"After Ponce de Leon arrived under the Spanish flag, it was the English conquerors of the 1700s who divided the peninsula into two territories, the 14th and 15th British colonies of the Americas," explains Cox. "They mapped everything, and gave land grants to Native Indians and new settlers. British Florida territories extended from around Myrtle Beach, South Carolina, southward and eastward to New Orleans, Louisiana; there were two Florida's divided by the St. Johns, Suwannee, and Apalachicola Rivers. Native Indians," according to Cox, "were destined to be 'missionized' by foreigners plundering through the New World."

When the British expanded their colonization in the 1600-1700's, Cox adds, "they set-up farms throughout Florida, bringing with them indentured servants from England who did not have money to pay the Lords in order to stay on their land; thus, it was go to the New Americas or go to prison."

From the 1600s, through three Seminole Indian Wars, ending in an unsettled peace in the 1800s, Native people attempted to hold onto their land grants and cattle but were eventually dispossessed, forced to move to Oklahoma reservations, or escape deep into the Everglades.

The Seminoles, who first settled in Florida in the 1700s, adds Cox, "became expert cowhandlers. One the most historic Seminole Indian Chiefs was called 'Cowkeeper,' who one time hosted naturalist/botanist William Bertram during his travels in Florida. Cowkeeper bestowed Bertram with his Native American name: 'Puc Puggy' or Flower Hunter."

William Bartram ventured into the southeast and Florida between 1773 and1776 as a lone explorer on horseback, he absorbed the natural world, studying and classifying native habitat. With a kind expression towards the Native people, he was graciously accepted into their circles recording, in their own "voices" stories about their culture and way of life.

Cox, a former quality assurance executive, has extensively researched records of Florida's earliest archeologists and historians. With a wild frontier heritage of ranchers, cattle rustlers, and confrontations with native people, Cox says author, Joe Ackerman wrote about one of the first "showdowns" between cowboys and Indians occurring as early as 1647. "But real beef production in the territories began when Jesuit and Franciscan Friars set up a network of Missions across north and north-central Florida," adds Cox. "The Missions served to convert Indians to Christianity, using them as labor to tend to their cattle. Some of the largest Spanish cattle holdings existed in Nassau County in 1698. Rancho de la Chua situated near what is now Payne's Prairie, Florida was run by relatives of Don Pedro Menendez de Aviles who founded Saint Augustine in 1565. The University of Florida in Alachua County was named after his ranch," adds Cox. It was during this period that British escaped slaves were migrating into Florida from the Carolinas and took jobs working cattle on Seminole lands, becoming the first "black cowboys."

"There were more than thirty privately owned 'ranchos' in Florida with a cattle count of about 2,000 head. However, the Spanish ranchers allowed their cattle and horses to graze wherever they pleased in conflict with those Indians who were pursuing an agrarian lifestyle; the Indians did not like the crop destruction." It was over "land" that stirred a rising uneasiness amongst new settlers and the Native population.

By the 1700s, the British colonists made their presence felt throughout the New World also as cattle ranchers. The British sailed across the Atlantic with a bulkhead of cattle breeds such as Gelb (Yellow), Durham, Kerry (Ireland), Hereford and Devon that they eventually crossed with "scrub cows" left behind by the Spaniards. "South Carolina became the main cattle range of the British colonies," says Cox.

"By 1702, British colonist James Moore and a group of militia volunteers accompanied by Creek Indians attacked northern Florida, during the raids on Spanish missions and forts. Most of the Spanish cattle were killed, creating a food hardship on settlers. The cattle that escaped fled into the swamps and woods where local Natives found them and began their own herds. The

Seminoles raised large herds of cattle on Payne's Prairie near Gainesville with Chief Billy Bowlegs and Cowkeeper grazing more than a 1000 head," explained Cox. "Later in 1704, British and Creek Indians virtually destroyed cattle raising in Spanish Florida. In the east Florida raids, Indians were denied guns by the Spanish and were helpless against Moore's militia. The troops devastated all of the land around Saint Augustine to Palatka. The Timucuan Indians in the area retreated to the Spanish fort; those who were not killed escaped or were taken to the Carolinas as slaves. It was later that these slaves escaped and returned back to Florida. They were called "Seminoles" from the Spanish word 'Cimarron,' meaning 'wild' or 'runaway.' The British also called the Creek Indian descendants 'Seminolies' or 'Seminoles.' Black slaves from the Carolinas joined the Seminoles around the 1750s and became the first 'Black Cowboys,'" added Cox. (See Chapter on "The Unconquered")

Despite Florida's tumultuous revolutionary history, there were also many natural disasters including earthquakes, hurricanes, and droughts with hostile takeovers continuing to be imminent. As colonization from Europe progressed, there were increased battles over the vast open rangeland and the areas of rich "black gold" farmland to nurture crops. "In the end, settlements were usually managed by the strongest conqueror," Cox explains.

However, for those adventurers who followed their dreams into the conquest of wild Florida they invented cures, remedies, and compounds for the various "maladies." In the 1700s, the new settlers had collected a wealth of new knowledge about the land and native species that grew into a guidebook recording information to help them build a life, grow food, treat illness/

disease, start businesses, "technology" and "industry" meaning in those days, how to be "industrious" or to survive. Moore's, *Universal Assistant, 1,000,000 Industrial Facts, Receipts, [recipes] calculations and C in Every Business and Engravings* was the "bible" on health, home and domicile. Various chapters offered "Farmers Receipts" on how to break and understand horse behaviors, deal with varmints and offered cures.

There was a chapter on "Death for Vermin on Plants or Animals." The recipe:

> Take 2 gallons of bowling hot water and one pound of tobacco leaves. Strain it 20 minutes for vermin and put it on animals/plants. This concoction is certain to kill vermin.

To preserve potatoes from rot:

> Pour lime on the floor 6 inches deep; put another layer of lime on the floor and dust it on the potatoes. This quill improves the flavor and kills fungi that causes rot.

There are many chapters on natural remedies. For a headache, a Parisian physician recommends a special compress mixing salt and ice together to place on the head for 1 minute.

Other remedies include:

> For a cold: Plunge the feet in mustard water to induce sweating; Mix 14 drops of camphor and white sugar in water and drink it. Freckles: Put 2 ounces of lemon, half a dram of borax, 1 dram of sugar in a container and let it ferment. Use this mixture occasionally on the face.

> Oriental cold cream: Take almonds and white wax, melt and add rosewater and orange flowers with "spermaceti," mix together and apply. ["Spermaceti from the Greek word sperma, seed, and cetus, is a wax extracted from whale oil that can be treated for use in cosmetics and other lubricants].

There is also the "magnetic bath, sheep dung cure, and how to make chloroform as an anesthetic. If you were treating "the croup," it called for crushed blood root, vinegar, and white sugar. For ear aches: Put 2 ounces of bruised garlic in oil of almond and let it set for a week then put it into the ear. [Perhaps this is the old "sweet oil" formula used to ease aches dating back to the 1940's].

In depth research by Cox on plant disease cures is also documented in James Adair's book, *The History of the American Indians, particularly those nations adjoining to the Mississippi, East and West Florida, Georgia, South and North Carolina, and Virginia,* originally published in 1775. Adair worked with the Cherokees, who Cox says had great knowledge about herbs and plants used as cures, although they did not have success curing small pox.

As Cox thumbs through the yellow-stained and well-worn pages of Moore's *Universal Assistant,* there are extensive directions on beekeeping. "The processes described in the book still remain as the longest established practices in the beekeeping industry today," says Cox.

Every one of the remedies was provided as a practical knowledge. Discovering how to use natural remedies and resources was a formidable task requiring patience, trial-and-error efforts, and eventually, expertise. The homesteaders created their own "technology," sophisticated for the time, as it was all there was. Building a log house, required trees that needed to be seasoned into lumber to survive harsh climatic changes. *The Universal Assistant* includes a chapter on "Lumbering and How to Season Timber."

As new English settlers and other Europeans continued to "people" the state, the 1800s revived unrest amongst the Seminole landholders. By 1813, General Andrew Jackson was ordered to go into the Florida territories to investigate any problems, which Cox says resulted "in another major Indian massacre." Turning his thoughts into history and another similar situation, Cox recalls the Battle at Wounded Knee Creek, the last major armed conflict between the Lakota Sioux, South Dakota and the United States comparing it to the plundering of General Andrew Jackson. Cox thinks "that if these massacres and atrocities had been publicized today, humanity would be outraged, but in those early days with nothing more than word-of-mouth, no one heard a peep. It is today's media exposure of every horrible global event that characterizes the world as a more violent place to live then when the New World was first settled." Nevertheless, in 1845, Florida became the 27th state to join the Union.

Rodney Miner and Don Cox are native Miamians who have known each other since 1954 when they both graduated from North Miami Senior High School, sharing a common interest in old relics that turned into a hobby. Today, the two "cow hunters" set up demonstrations on "living" Florida history at various state festivals, showing people lien-to "cow camps," how cattlemen lived on cross-state "cracker trails" driving thousands of cattle to coastal markets.

Rodney Miner says that "people today don't know much about the 'cow camps.' In our display, we show hides of opossums, gators, turkeys, foxes, otters, and other animals used as barter for beef and staples between trappers and cattlemen along the trails. Every part of the animal was used either for food or hides to make clothing and other necessities."

Don Cox was born in Brooklyn, New York. At four months, Cox and his mother moved to his Aunt's house in Miami while his father served as a Marine in World War II and the Korean War. The family left Miami around 1951 and returned in 1954.

Don Cox served in Air Force Intelligence as a government contractor, 1993-2001 in Saudi Arabia. Documenting historical markers King Abdul Asis ibn Saud, united the tribes of 'Arabia' under one King into the 'United Arab Tribes.' Islam was used to control people by a designated force called the religious police of 'matowas.' In the New World on the North American continent, missions were used by Britain and Spain in the same way to control and convert Indians and settlers. What happened in Saudi Arabia happened here."

One particular incident Cox recalls regarding the "matowas" in Saudi Arabia occurred when he had been in the country for four months. Cox was told by a military confidante that "eight hundred rebellious soldiers and 'matowas' where boarded onto a C-120 aircraft that reached a cruising altitude of 13,000 feet. The soldiers were then asked to 'pledge allegiance to the King' or take a walk out the back door out of the aircraft." Cox, who says he is a devout Christian, believes"the United States needs to stop getting involved in deeply religious conflicts, as others like the way they live."

"Religious wars have occurred in many country histories," Cox reflects. On June 28, 1914, Archduke Franz Ferdinand, heir to the Austro-Hungarian throne, and his wife Sophie were killed point blank by Gavrilo Princip in Sarajevo when they were leaving a reception. It was this event that triggered the outbreak of war in Europe," and with a finality adds, "This is just how it is."

Miner, whose fondness for native culture dates back to his Boy Scout days says he learned the Indian way of life from his boyhood expeditions. "I liked being close to nature, swimming in lakes, rivers, and hunting. One of my most meaningful life experiences was learning survival skills at the Boy Scout camp in the Everglades."

"The Scout Master prepared us for our adventure into the Glades and told us that we could bring one weapon to hunt for food; I chose my 22 rifle." As the troop hiked into the dense swamp, Miner, his mentor, and companions began to forage through the mucky slush hunting for game or fish. Miner says he spotted the streak of a garfish and took it as his first prize. After the hunters tracked their prey, they returned to the evening campfire with a motley collection of turtles and other small creatures that all went into the dinner stew.

As Miner grew into the role of a hunter, but not for trophies, he learned to skin and tan pelts and not to waste any part of the animal. Today, Miner uses this skill crafting by-products from animal skins into leather for pouches, pelts, and purses.

After a tour of duty in the Army during the Viet Nam crisis, Miner returned to hometown Miami and worked as a land surveyor for 30 years. Then a long-time friend, who worked in the Broward County Historical Society, invited Miner to demonstrate the art of hide tanning at the County fair. This was his first public debut displaying the talent he honed many years before as a Boy Scout.

Miner and Cox are "time travelers" taking people back to an era, distant from today, when people lived off the land and by their own survival skills. Through research and actualizing that past in their replication of Florida pioneer days, Miner and Cox have evolved a wisdom and philosophy into lessons learned as a rule of thumb for today. "I don't think people can change much about what's going on," reflects Miner. "Politicians may initially have good intentions, but there is always change, then new faces and ideas appear. Yet, it all sounds the same; the same old speeches that don't make a particle of difference," Miner emphasizes. "I believe in living my life by how I think I should live it with a standard of integrity, honor, honesty, and truthfulness. This is how I raised my children and influence my grandchildren. I'm sorry to see all of the so-called 'progress' called urban 'villages' developing where wilderness, farmland, and hunting landscapes used to be, but today are deemed, not by Nature's standards but man's, as 'not functional.' Nature's concept of 'usefulness' is far different from man's. Man does not value the native scrub; it is said to be 'dysfunctional' and that the land can be better used for other purposes. Man is growing away from himself and losing touch with Nature."

How do Cox and Miner strive to bring awareness to people to appreciate Nature? "Programs like the Boy Scouts," says Miner, "and pioneer festivals such as those held in Leesburg, Dade City, and Kissimmee expose the public to living history with the camps and cowboy poets. My grandson's mother says to him that he needs to spend more time outdoors, so what does he do, he goes outdoors and takes the computer." In another example, Miner says he was discussing behavior problems in school with a teacher who attributes these problems directly to lack of parental involvement in children's lives. "Parents don't know what their children are doing due to the fast lifestyle and working several jobs. It is a dilemma."

How is the cycle broken? Miner believes by refocusing on a "quality of life" as a priority. To make "sense" of misplaced priorities, he quotes an old adage: "One has not experienced life until he has faced danger. Life has a flavor that the protected will never know. I catch rattlesnakes with my hands. Why? I am after the hide and meat. Sometimes the rattlers I catch I release and often they do not rattle or attempt to strike, only get away. They are not always aggressive. But, one old timer told me that if he sees a rattlesnake, he kills it, but not Rodney Miner, I move it."

Today, Miner takes care of cattle for an absentee owner near Inverness. He helps load cows, feed, and castrate bulls in exchange for grazing his horses on the land. But the cattle business is rift with close-calls and humorous catastrophes. "Last year there was a crop of new bulls, each about 150 pounds that were scheduled to be castrated," says Miner. "My partner, Paul Anderson, usually does the cut while I hold down the bull on his side. In this case, Anderson made the first cut, I was in the front and we needed to switch positions but the bull's adrenalin kicked-in a big way and knocked both of us off. We had to re-catch the bull not to leave him loose and injured. We needed to finish the job." Miner says when they finally re-recaptured the very angry bull they had to struggle to complete the cut. When it was over and they released the "steer," he described himself in the words of an old "cow hunter" axiom: "I was up to my boots tops in manure, blood and mud!" These are just some of the everyday challenges early pioneers had to endure and conquer, to survive.

"Why do I do this?" Miner asks himself. "I'm doing things our Florida ancestors did. many years ago. Today, there are city types who never think of researching the past, going out into the wild and being deeply involved in a similar way. Awhile back my son-in-law came to visit from New York with his 12 year old daughter. Well, we got out there in the woods where the dogs cornered a barren sow; they had chewed pretty badly on her ear and neck. The sow was injured so I had to dispatch the sow by using my folding knife to slit the hog's throat." Miner explains that "as Nature took its course, the lifeblood of the hog flowed and mixed with the swamp water." Back at the evening campfire when everyone was feasting on fresh barbecued pork, Miner says the little girl looked up at him with innocence in her words: "Mr. Miner, I didn't know you knew you had to do that on a hog hunt. My son-in-law even commented that he didn't know I could do such a 'dastardly' deed."

HANK MATSON: THE HYMN OF THE COWBOY POET

One of a kind, cowboy poet, Hank Matson is a man born apart from the cultural era in which he emulates today. Looking like 1800s "cow hunter" Jake Summerlin at the "Kowtown Festival" wearing a lasso looped at his side, tall boots, and a 10 gallon Stetson, he is an anachronism, stepping from the pages of the past into the 21st Century. In his "saddlebag" of personal repertoires, he carries a collection of original stories that still capture the listener today just as it did over two hundred years ago when tired and weary "cow hunters" ended a long cattle drive beneath a canopy of stars around the campfire. Matson says he has been collecting stories all of his life but in the 1990's he starting telling them to the public.

It all happened when he says he "sat too close to the campfire and someone said, 'It's your turn to tell a story.' This is how it all started." Matson has performed at the Douglasville, Georgia; Prescott, Arizona and Kanab, Utah cowboy poetry gatherings and all over Florida. Today, he entertains young and old with traditional stories of pioneer days when they brought their tales of adventure back to the campfire as the night's entertainment. "Bone Mizell who lived 1863-1920 is my hero," says Matson. He lived in Arcadia and died as a drunk, who is not me, but he did what I want to do: Ride all day without ever seeing a fence or telephone wire."

Mattson, who lives in Lake Placid, describes his mission in the traditional language of a poet:

> "Sort suitable fer pert near any audience, my own work and those
> of turn-of-the century cow punchers com together to chronicle
> and preserve the life and times of the myriad of Florida folks who
> nearly for 400 years have been workin' cattle. Some audiences
> have laughed and cried, tohers have been enlightened. A few have
> been educated and informed, and while I don't mean to brag, the
> instance has been known when insomnia suffers have amazingly
> been cured."

One of Matson's favorite stories he relates to kids:

> "If you could hear a cow speak this is what I would tell ya."
> I am a cow; hear me "moo." I make milk and cream for you,
> zesty cheese, and sweet butter and in the end, I am hamburger
> meat. This is the story of life."

Matson works cattle at the Rockin' JS Ranch owned by the Scott brothers in Avon Park where they raise Brangus cows. He says that the old days of the "cow hunter" are gone, but not dead. "The cattle industry in Florida is not dying, as there is a great demand for beef." Matson explains that the cattle business is becoming very hi-tech and today you have to learn new ranching technology. Now Global Positioning Satellites (GPS) are part of the business, along with new 21st Century research conducted at Buck Island in Lake Placid, and on the Brighton Seminole Reservation in Okeechobee. It is exciting. A young person, who wants to work cows, can help out cattlemen on one of the large ranches, like the biggest one in the Unlisted States, the Deseret Ranch in Brevard County. It is difficult today to find people who want to work cows."

"In Florida, the small mom and pop ranches are still around, but unless a ranch is inherited, it is very expensive to start-up in the business due to high property prices; today, the land is worth more than the cattle. Although small ranches are disappearing, the legend of the 'cow hunter' is very much alive worldwide." Matson adds that it will be a very sad day if "the United States

The DeBarys' at the Kowtown Festival Kissimmee, Florida

has to import beef from foreign countries. It would be a definite tragedy."

A FAMILY TRADITION

Dressed as a Miccosukee Indian at the "Kowtown Festival," Earl DeBary's grandfather Samuel Frederick originally came to America as a "moonshine champagne" dealer settling north of Orlando in the 1820s.

Moving from New York to Florida, the elder DeBary had a fleet of steamships plying the St. John's River, alongside 9,000 acres of land where he constructed a traditional colonial mansion. DeBary humbly called the Mansion his "hunting lodge" where some fifty years ago, he hosted a distinguished list of Presidents, Kings and Princes.

Debary's grandfather was a Seminole, originally of the Muskogee and Creek Indian tribe of Georgia. The family migrated to Florida, says DeBary, "to get away from the 'white man.'"

Alongside her husband, Bettie DeBarry bustles around the cook fire as a 1830s Seminole lady. The couple has studied over twelve years, the life and teachings of the Seminoles living as well in a chickee at Silver Springs. "Our purpose is to interpret a 'living history,' to share the cultural heritage with others." Born in Williston, Bettie's pioneer father Rufus Halsett and her granddaddy Peter Hale, settled in Marion County in 1837. Today, the DeBarys' continue to provide the public with their living lessons of old Florida

PART II

KEEPING THE LEGEND ALIVE: FLORIDA CRACKER HERITAGE

ELEVEN

TWO HUNDRED YEARS OF TRADITION: THE GREAT FLORIDA CATTLE DRIVE OF OUGHT 6

The 1800s cattle drives are carved deeply into the legends of Florida history when "cow hunters" drove their herds over hundred of miles on the old "cracker trail" to markets in Punta Rassa, shipping them aboard paddle boats to Cuba and Key West to replenish the beef supply after the Civil and Spanish American Wars, and by train from Ft. Pierce north to the breadbasket of the country.

Marked by long days over rutted, dusty trails, through swamps and across Lake Okeechobee and the Kissimmee River, skilled horsemen along with their faithful cur dogs, gathered together in the annual round-up to minister to their trade. Working thousands of cattle across Florida, camping along the way for weeks at a time, the "cow hunters" settled down nightly in encampments, greeted at dusk by the welcome waft of hot vittles (sometimes entrails) cooked up on an open fire minded by the chuck wagon "chef" that lured their tired and dusty bones back to the cow camp to hunker down for the night beside their brooding herd. The clank of tin cups and the lowing cows echoed into sunset as the glowing embers slowly sank into nightfall and the "cow hunters" marked the close of day. Resting upon saddles and blankets, the great story tellers began their art of warming the spirit, weaving together an oral history of humorous stories collected along the way, spun around the campfire with some songs, as the sun melted into the horizon and night settled over fading embers into a canopy of stars.

In the fast pace of the 21st Century, those long ago years were once again revived and relived as participants gathered together to memorialize the "cow hunter" heritage and bring to life those deeply etched pages of history across the long Florida "cracker trails."

Commemorating the drive of 95 and the cow culture history, the Great Florida Cattle Drive of Ought 6 began in Osceola County December 5th, and wound up at the final watering hole in Kenansville, December 9th with more than 480 native "cracker" cattle and 600 "cow punchers" of all ages and occupations guided in by handpicked "Circle Bosses," (identified by their colored bands assigned by geographic regions in Florida) to the Silver Spurs Arena. As the crew came

Mike Wilder and Andrew Bower

into sight along a tree lined horizon on the last leg of the ride, the snaps of cracking whips, scrambling hooves and guttural mooing cows were greeted by the hoots and hollers of fans, families and curious onlookers as Cow Boss, Mike Wilder and Seminole Tribal Leader Andrew Bowers led the herd home on the fifth and final day of the trek.

Booming over a loudspeaker across the prairie, pioneer rancher and cattle drive organizer Doyle Conner, Jr., provided a colorful dialog of history and noteworthy events that filled in lost memories of those by-gone days when the trail ride was a means of livelihood for pioneer cow culture families who gave birth to the Florida cattle industry. "You can hear the whips in the distance, three cracks, you're in a hurry; a pause, and three cracks and you're in trouble; or, a family rhythm might develop that just means it's time for lunch, but, the 'cracker whip' is a tool of the trade," said Conner. And, as the cattle weaved across the prairie to the last "encampment" there were plenty of expert "whip crackers" who demonstrated their popping skills, said to exceed the sound barrier at the end of the snap.

The Cattlemen's Frolic, celebrating the end of the ride, included historical reenactments of the past, cow camp exhibits, vendors selling cowboy paraphernalia, pioneer books, and there were good old fashioned barbecue ribs. For a variety of entertainment, there was the bank robbery, cowboy poets, cracker crooners and an art auction featuring artists from the Cowboy Artists Association of Florida. Among many others were Benjamin Dehart a.k.a. "the Cracker Crooner" from Orlando who camped along the trail and provided old Florida tunes, as well as fifth generation Winter Haven resident,

Jerry Mincey singer/and "cracker" song writer. Long time cowboy poet Hank Matson, attired in his full regalia, and whose native history is deeply embedded in Florida, brought to the foreground a barrage of collected stories masterfully presented with a unique "cracker" humor reflecting the lifestyle of the early pioneers. Gary McMahan from Colorado was on hand to "wow" the crowd with his songs, poems, stories, barn burning yodels and his great new song "Okeechobee Joe" inspired by former FCA President, Joe Pearce. This first class entertainer was sponsored by the FCA.

As part of the historical tradition at the nightly encampments when riders spread their blankets on the ground, a depiction of the "way it was," included reviving Florida's historical past from the times of the early Timucuan Indian culture, the Spanish Colonial possession, Seminole and Civil Wars, lest those times be forgotten.

The Cowboy Artist Association of Florida had many of its members displaying original artwork of Florida's cow culture. Storytellers, re-enactors and demonstrators at the old-fashioned 'FROLIC" gave visitors a first hand look into Florida's ranching heritage and cow culture traditions. Dismounting from the ride, wearing a buckskin skirt and fringed vest, Desiree Mufson of Stuart, expressed her strong sense of appreciation for the traditions of the early pioneers and her connection to the past, after her first experience on the trail. "I felt a sense of history, as if the present did not exist." Long time rancher, Iris Wall, owner of the Seminole Inn in Indiantown and lifelong friend, Mildred Sherrod of Immokalee, reminisced about their lives and experiences that they said have given them humor and calamity surviving in the cattle industry. In a setting far off the beaten path of the Orlando urban corridor, the Silver Spurs Arena at Kenansville is the home of the Heartbreak

Hotel, the old bank and post office that was plucked down again at its old site after a preservation respite on the Adams Ranch in Ft. Pierce.

The success of the trail ride is attributed to many sponsors and supporters, said Conner. The Seminole Tribe provided the cattle power and colorful traditions for the event wearing their customary handmade attire. Besides visitors, there was not a "green horn" in sight as buckskin, chaps, boots and hats were the traditional dress of the day. There were no T-shirts, tennis shoes or ball caps

Pioneer "cow huntresses" Iris Wall and Mildred Sherrod

allowed at the historical event. Doyle Conner tipped his hat to the many participants and sponsors including the Florida Agricultural Museum, The Florida Cattlemen's Association, Eli's Western Wear, Florida Ranchland Realty, The Property Owners, Seminole Feeds of Ocala, and the Florida Department of Agriculture and Consumer Services.

Doyle Conner

At the end of the day, as the orange glow of the sun once again settled behind the scrub prairie, the guttural sounds of cows, the occasional whine of a horse, and the waft of fresh vittles cooking on an open fire closed the gap of time from those olden, golden days when the "cow hunter" his horse, and his dog, rode into the night along the wide open range across Florida.

The echo of a bard owl wafts upon the wind,
Silence descends like dew on tall cabbage palms,
Silver clouds shadow the Moon.
Silhouetted beneath the stars is two hundred years of heritage,
As the "cow hunter" hunkers down beside his brooding herd.
Here, Time stands still...
Lingering upon the precipice of the Future.

Nancy Billie and Sarafina Rose

TWELVE

THE UNCONQUERED SEMINOLES

The Seminole people are a tribe of many cultural traditions. The Seminoles began to trickle into Florida in the 1700s settling around Payne's Prairie near Gainsveille with the lower Creek Indians from Georgia bulding their villages and farms along the high ridges near Lake Okeechobee today called "Indiantown." Along with other Southern tribes, the Indians became known as "Seminoles" derived from the word "Myskoke" of the Creek language and "simino-li, an adaptation of the Spanish word "Cimarron" which meant to Europeans: "Wild or "wild men."

The Seminoles began to round up "scrub cattle" left behind by the Spanish in the 1500s and to build their own herds. However, as more Europeans filtered into Florida, unrest grew between Seminoles and new settlers who were moving into desirable rangelands of their territory. The rift over land was the basis for the First Seminole War (1817-1818) led by U.S. Army General Andrew Jackson.

In 1821, when Spain ceded Florida to the United States, Indians were forced to leave their Territory and move to an Oklahoma reservation, some refused, resulting in the passage of the Indian Romoval Act of 1830, resulting in the Second Seminole War (1835-43). During the same period, northern Black slaves were escaping their captors. The Blacks did not want to go back to the plantation and Seminoles did not want to go to the reservation, thus, many escaped slaves teamed up with the Seminoles. Some of the Blacks lived in separate groups but fought alongside the Seminoles to hold onto the land and cattle. Colonel Zachary Taylor and more than a thousand troops tramped along the Kissimmee River from Tampa to raid the Indians with orders to destroy or capture any that remained.

After fighting through years of the Seminole War, Seminole leader, Chief Osceola was taken prisoner at Fort Moutrie, South Carolina and never saw the light of freedom again. He died incarcerated in 1838, but other Seminole leaders led by warriors Micanopy, Alligator, and Jumper defeated the onslauught of soldiers using "guerella warfare." One Union soldier commissioned to hunt down Indians in the heavily mosquito and snake invested swamps said that if "he had to chose Hell or Florida, he would chose Hell!"

After the Third Seminole War (1855-58), forts were constructed acrross Florida armed with bounty hunters to capture remaining Indians and move them to Oklahoma. Bounty hunters were paid $500 for warriors, $250 for women, and $200 for children. Colonel Taylor plotted and built outposts across twenty mile grids. With great fortitude, the remaining Seminoles traipsed deeper into the Everglades, adapted to harsh conditions and learned to survive off the land. Many Seminoles hid in the swamp for years before feeling safe enough to emerge. This small group of couragous Seminoles never surrendered.

In the 21st Century, the Seminole traditions are a living heritage. Young Matthew Griffin, 16, garbed in turn-of-the-century Indian attire at the Kowtown Festival in Kissimmee, says his heritage dates back to the 1800s in Hernando County when his family became part of the Seminole tribe. Griffin says he "feels Seminole." Surrounded by people he tells his story. "You can't understand who you are, and where to go, unless you know where you came from," remarks Griffin. This is Griffin's quest.

Delving into early history, Griffin says there were approximately a thousand slaves in the 1830s that lived in Seminole villages. "John Horse was one of the greatest Muscogee Indians of his day. He learned to speak English and spoke Hitachi as well, acting as an interpreter," says Griffin. "The slaves and the Indians came together for a common goal: To be free and break the aggressive power of the government," adds Griffin. The escaped Black slaves

helped to foster Seminole Indian cattle trade.

Moses Osceola, President of today's Florida Seminole Tribe, a replication of the long days and nights that wound into Kenansville, remembering the days when "cow hunters" drove thousands of cattle to east and west coast markets on the old "cracker trails" carved across Central Florida. Osceola emphasizes that "the Seminole people have always been engaged in raising cattle, expanding later years into citrus and gaming." According to Osceola, "the main thrust of the Seminole tribe is to preserve the cultural heritage by teaching children the Miccosukee language and history. It is important to continue all traditions and enterprises for the tribe to survive. Many of the traditions are not found in history books." Moses Osceola grew up on the Hollywood reservation and has been working cattle since high school. He works to incorporate new business development into enterprises for the survival of the Tribe.

Echoing the importance of Seminole traditions, an Elder woman says that traditions are a sacred practice held only within the tribe. It is the role of the woman to teach the ways of wisdom to their family."

Another important designation within the Tribe is the Medicine Man who holds a place of honor as spiritual practitioner and protector of sacred ceremonies and healing. "The Medicine Man must earn this position or 'ahwneechh' (wake-up in to his role) and be approved by the Tribe in order to practice the many secret rituals. He learns these practices from older men," says Elder Jimmie Osceola. "The Seminole beliefs are based on spiritual values handed down from the 'Creator' as written in the Bible. God created the Earth and we came out with it. The Seminole knowledge of the Medicine is not to be revealed outside of the Tribe."

If a tribal member decides to consult a traditional doctor outside the tribe, it is said that the diagnosis is brought back to the Medicine Man for his direction and prescription. However, "for a healing to occur," adds Jimmie Osceola, "the Medicine must be practiced exactly as directed. Some of these directions may prescribe the drinking of special sacred herbs."

During the sacred marriage ceremony, the Medicine Man gives the bride and groom "traditional herbs to regurgitate, to purify the body before the union. At birth, new born babies receive their Indian name from the Medicine Man, but the young also receive an English name," explains Osceola.

Revealing only a few scant details, Osceola says the Medicine Man anoints the "Corn Dance" for harvest and conducts funeral rites. "A person who dies is placed on a platform with stilts and covered with a blanket," describes Osceola.

Jimmie Osceola, born in 1931 into the Panther Clan, grew up on the Brighton Reservation and lived there his entire life. As a boy he went to the Seminole Indian School and attended cattle. During his teen years, Osceola was not drafted for the Viet Nam War although many young Seminoles volunteered; however, he adds that "there were not enough Indian boys left on the reservation."

Osceola's wife Gloria is from the Miccossukee Tribe that settled in South Florida (the Miccossukees did not join the Florida Seminole Nation). "The Missosukees remains independent, strongly attached to practicing old traditions," says Osceola.

The Osceola's' have four children, three boys and a girl. Today, enjoying the traditional Brighton Rodeo events, he lives happily in retirement on the reservation and leaves behind lingering words of wisdom: We learn to watch Nature, not the calendar. In March, the tips of the trees and plants begin their new growth. This is how we look at life. Go to church and work like everyone else. What more can you do?"

At the annual Field Days at Brighton Seminole Reservation, Wilse Brulsedhead of the Alberta, Canada "Blood Tribe" is a 23 year old calf roper. Brulsedhead, a member of the Professional Cowboy and Rodeo Association (PCRA) is part of the Eastern Indian Rodeo Association. Behind the grandstand, waiting for his grand entrance into the arena, with one arm he swirls his rope and with the other rocks his young child in a stroller.

The annual event also features the crowning of "Miss Florida Seminole" and "Little Miss Seminole." In 2007-2008, Jennifer Chalfant, 19 is honored to wear the Miss Florida Seminole crown and Little Miss Seminole is Brianna Bowers, age 6.

THIRTEEN

COWBOYS RULE IN DOWNTOWN OKEECHOBEE

CELEBRATING
"NATIONAL DAY OF THE COWBOY"

On a blistering summer day when Highway 70 is usually bustling with traffic, road blocks were posted to temporarily halt the flow of cars and trucks to make way for a stately procession of cracker cows, cowboys, and wagons led by a "posse" of Sheriff's Deputies rambling out of the pages of Florida history into downtown Okeechobee making its way to the Ag Center, the staging of the National Day of the Cowboy, July 28, 2007.

Kicking off the day sponsored by the Okeechobee Cattleman's Association, the Seminole Tribe, Main Street, Eli's Western Wear and other contributors, spectators lined the streets to watch "real" cowboys herding along cracker cows as children laughed, and cameras clicked with reporters scurrying ahead of the herd to capture scenes re-lived from Okeechobee's early "cow town" days. Leading the procession of cowboys and cattle were Ephriam and Alfred Norman, Pete Clemons, Buddy Adams, Larry Rooks, Charlie Bronson, Haynes Williams and Roland Durrance.

After the procession ended at the Ag arena, events inside began. The legendary Gordie Peer demonstrated his whip cracking prowess and the crowd laughed along with Doyle Rigdon, cowboy poet and storyteller. The highlight of the day was the "ranch rodeo" where local ranchers teamed up to demonstrate their daily skills in a friendly competition. Everything from team doctoring, calf-branding, "wild cow" milking was part of the day's agenda. At the end of the day, the Freedom Ranch with Elton and Angela Boney, Matt Davis, Weston Pryor and Heath Crumb took away the top honor as winners of the Ranch Rodeo.

Outside the arena, visitors had the opportunity to stroll around at booths

and talk to professional cowboys who displayed their special talents in making the everyday "tools of the trade." Mike Wilder, who was honored as a "Cow Boss" in the 2006 Cattledrive across Osceola County, has been a cowboy all his life and has specialized for the past thirty years in making customized Western saddles. He had several hand-made saddles at his booth and provided visitors with insight into a vernacular vocabulary of the "swell," "the tree" and the "standard bar" that Mike accesses in matching horse and rider to the saddle. Although Mike inherited his saddlemaking tools, he went to a South Dakota school for seven months to perfect the art. Mike also graduated from Texas Christian University (TCU) in Ranch Management.

There was the "Cowhunter Congress," Florida history presented through a hands-on artifact collection of Joyce Rawlins and Sally Carlton Breaux. One of the well-worn cowboy hats on display still retained the shape and embedded rings of toil from its former owner.

Buddy Mills, whose "cow hunter" heritage dates back generations, learned

the art of "building" cracker whips from his daddy. Buddy says his daddy made his first whip when he was 15 years old using the tops of tall discarded boots for leather strings to braid, then whittled the handles himself. Buddy said "as long as my hands let me, I will continue making whips." The one whip that his daddy did not finish, Buddy preserves as a special commemoration "to the master."

One man, a living "cow hunter" legend and war hero, talked about the days of the Texas Rangers. Allen Adams, 86, was born in Friendship, Texas and worked cattle on the open range that he said was not too different from

Florida. Adams fought in World War II, landing with the Second Infantry on D-Day in Normandy. There was a display of the many distinguished medals Adams received during five campaigns across Europe from 1943-45. In one particularly difficult time, Adams recalls almost drowning when landing on the beach weighted down with all the heavy gear; however, fortunately he survived that event and the war.

July 28th was an old fashioned "hootenanny" of barbeque beef, brisket, hot dogs, ice cream and cold drinks and a real-life education that reminds those who stopped here on this hot summer Saturday that the "cowboy way" is still alive and well, not only in Okeechobee and Florida but is part of America's heritage honored on this day.

FOURTEEN

"BUCKIN' BULLS":
INDIAN RIVER COUNTY HORSE TRAINER AND CLINICIAN
DAVE TRAPHAGEN

"Bulls love to Buck," says Dave Traphagen of Doublehooked Horsemanship who has been riding bulls and training riders for more than forty years. In

1969, he had the World Champion Reining horse, "Nifty Della Bee" and played polo as a hobby. Today, as a horse trainer and clinician at his Indian River County facility, he still rides bulls at least once a year when he's not working with rising buckin' bull rodeo stars.

"Bulls today," says Traphagen, "are bred for athleticism; born to buck. Although they do slow down after about twelve years, in their growth period they love to buck just as much as the riders who love the challenge. It takes a lot to stay on two tons of solid muscle in the rodeo arena for those long 8 seconds."

Traphagen studies the big animals to understand their moves and strengths but says they also have unique personalities. "There is one bull I used to feed a carrot to right from my mouth. He could be as gentle as a pet until he hit the alleyway of the arena, then he would hook or trample anyone who got in his way. Well-known and respected Texas stock contractor, Terry Williams says of his bull, "Cripple Creek Promised Land" the 1999 bull of the year that "he was so easy going you could put a Santa Claus hat on him. Even championship rider, Tuff Hedermen, put his 7 year old boy on 'Promised Land' and walked him around the pasture like a gentle horse. But when that bull hit the arena gate, his mind set would change and he became a fierce challenge for any rider."

As a Professional Bull Rider judge and respected horseman, Traphagen has been a cowboy since a young boy participating in various rodeo events from calf roping to bull riding but says the rodeo business has changed over the years. He says today there are more animal rights groups disparaging the use of horses and cows in some rodeo events adding that "urbanization of Florida is displacing cowboys from making a living in the traditional way, working cows. With the gradual extinction of the small family ranch, a cowboy has to work now on one of the remaining larger spreads. If he can't find work there, he has to find another job."

Yet, the romanticism of the "cowboy" is still alive today in legend, if not in practice. "The cowboy who remains a 'cowboy' is a new American hero," says Traphagen. "The rodeo sport grew out of the ranching business since the days of the old Florida 'cracker trails' when thousands of cattle were herded across state to coastal markets. Cowboys from surrounding ranches would join together for the long rides, camping along the way trailed by the chuckwagon cook. They lived in the open, endured torrential rains, mosquitoes, and blistering summer sun for weeks at a time. The family stayed behind to take care of the ranch and garden planted for their livelihood."

However, "the 'cowboy way' reflects a larger image," Traphagen describes. "The 21st Century cowboy lives a tradition of personal values. He is soft-spoken, respects women, and never lies. He is a gentleman, courteous, and believes in God. I do all I can to promote 'the cowboy way' which is disappearing in Florida." Traphagen wants to "keep alive the tradition of bull-riding, one of the fastest growing rodeo competitions. The future of championship bull riders is promising, as the purses of the Professional Cowboy and Rodeo Association (PCRA) have risen to $20-30,000 per event. The prize money draws the best professional cowboys from all over the world attracting young men from as far away as Australia, Mexico, and Canada. Today the competition is tough competing against top pros like Adrian Morales from San Carlos, Brazil, one of the best bull riders in the world."

For the young at heart who follow their dreams from rodeos city to city, traveling across country in long-neck trucks camping with horses, rope, and gear are those that pursued their burning desire at an early edge on the back of a calf, as Traphagen did when he was 6 years old. The bull riders learn to perfect their ability, matching human skill and wit against animal instinct. Today, Traphagen travels to rodeo events throughout the state with his mechanical bull, instructing hopeful youths on how to stay on the stationery "buckin' bull" for those breathtaking 8 seconds. Young and old "bull ridin' wanna' bes" mount up on the saddle with sideline cheers from family and friends with the excitement as real as if the bull was the infamous, "Promised Land" in the rodeo arena.   Traphagen coaches riders to hold their hand high, grip with the knees, lean into the bull's neck and to stay lifted. A few daring riders will ask Traphagen to "turn up the juice" which often leads to a bouncing dismount onto the padded arena. However, the ride ends, despite the dismount, patrons leave with a laugh and sense of pride because they can say "I have ridden a buckin' bull."

Born in Columbus, Ohio, the family raised and trained show horses. But Dave Traphagen and his brother Scott, raised by their physician father, had a different path they wanted to pursue. "My daddy did not want his sons to be cowboys. He warned us of the risks of injuries as professional bull riders," says Traphagen. But, despite the odds, the brothers prevailed and pursued their career. Following in the footsteps of the Traphagen brothers, Dave works to provide scholarships for young rodeo riders to compete in local circuits and help them fulfill their dream. He takes the mechanical bull to various schools to teach morale building and confidence. "The kids always come off the bull grinning with self-esteem and learning something new." Traphagen also has Team Rodeo as a sponsor to put together hats and shirts for sale that supports injured cowboys and helps pay for entry fees. As a cowboy himself, Traphagen supports the sport as lasting tradition and says: "My heroes have always been cowboys."

EPILOGUE

OLD FLORIDA IN THE 21ST CENTURY

PRESERVING OLD FLORIDA

ROXANNE AND DUSTY YOUNG

SEBRING

More than a century ago when wild cracker cows left by Spanish conquistadors roamed the prairie grasslands, Florida offered a new life for immigrants who traveled into the peninsula in buckboards loaded down with all of their belongings, family, traveling with a herd of cattle. When they found a place to settle down in the uncharted wilderness, they began the arduous chore of homesteading. The newcomers cut and honed timber to build log houses adapted to Florida heat with a "dog trot" carved down the center where breezes freely flowed, opening onto wide verandas across the front and back with a floating swing creaking in the wind. They found the place their dreams possessed in a virgin land where the stars hung low from the dark sky and the cows lowed contentedly grazing in the wide open spaces. These days are passed, but not forgotten. On the edge of rapidly growing Sebring in the heartland of Florida, those bygone days have been painstakingly recreated in the 21st Century by Roxanne and Dusty Young in Highlands County.

Dusty Young's granddaddy came to Florida in 1928 settling in Moore Haven as a carpenter. Harold Young built just this kind of house on the land he homesteaded. He was a rugged individualist that hunted alligator, deer, and turkey in the jungle hammocks of the Everglades prairies. He built swamp buggies to ply through thick saw grass and fire buggies that cut a swath though blazing wildfires. The family settled in Sebring. When Dusty's daddy was a "cow man" working cattle just like he did all his life for various ranchers.

Dusty was born in 1959 where he learned to take care of the land, raise horses, and do all that was necessary on the ranch. For fifteen years, Dusty roped and worked cows until he met Roxanne who became his wife. Roxanne was a barrel racer, rode western pleasure and showed horses. The couple shared many common interests through their love of horses and the land. After the two married, they began to create their own dreams of building a ranch, raising quarter horses and cattle on an open piece of land that was once part Chess Skippers six townships.

Dusty Young learned new ways of ranching he incorporated into the old "tried and true" practices. "Today there are improved pastures, not the same as the rough woods burned off by early 'cow hunters' for cattle grazing." Young knows the old ways of making a living from the land but today he is on the fringes of the urban setting in Sebring. However, Young still gigs frogs, hunts, fishes and catches moccasins in palmetto roots. He is a skilled sportsman. Recalling, "the way it was" in old Florida, Young says that "as time passed, cattlemen expanded their enterprise from cattle into citrus which today covers thousands of acres in Florida." But the Young's' put forth their strongest

Roxanne Young and her new foal

interest in ranching, living close to the land, and most recently, building their "cracker" dream home.

"We researched every aspect of old 'cracker' homes and duplicated as close as possible how those early log houses were built. We wanted to live as authentically as the pioneers did when they first settled carved out settlements on the land," Roxanne explains.

Looking out from the wide vista of the veranda as cows contentedly lull in the pastures and Roxanne's newest foal learns to stand on wobbly legs, there is not an urban intrusion in the line of sight; no street light pollution or noise, only the distant call of songbirds flocking overhead.

The Young's' hand-built house has been featured in *Southern Living Magazine* and newspaper articles but more than anything depicted in print, the house is lived in as a home reflecting 21st Century modern comforts but in the pride and spirit of preserving "old Florida."

ESCAPE TO GLADES COUNTY IN FLORIDA'S LAST PRISTINE WILDERNESS

A soft breeze feathers through thatches of palmettos spiking a crimson horizon, as dragonflies "toe-dance" from peak to peak, flashing their turquoise iridescence along a whimsical path. Beams of sunlight stream through waving cabbage palms tracing their graceful stalks into native scrub. Quietly, the morning awakes in this small crevasse of Glades County, nestled on the western shore of Lake Okeechobee in the vast Everglades prairie; a living spectacle of Nature's unobtrusive Beauty that captures the senses and stamps its unique imprint upon space, time, and those who carry their weary bodies from the bustle of city drama into the fresh air of the pristine wilderness.

Traveling from the coast about 35 miles along Highway 80 West (Southern Boulevard) through South Bay, the road curves northwest on U.S. 27 towards Clewiston, named after Alonso Clewis, who founded the first sugar company when he discovered that cane grew well in the "black-gold muck" along the southern tip of Lake Okeechobee (the second largest fresh water lake in the nation). In the heart of Clewiston is the majestic Clewiston Inn built in 1938, reflecting the southern charm and hospitality of the 1900s "boom days" when tourists visited from all over the world seeking adventure in wild Florida. The

Inn, on the National Register of Historic Sites, serves breakfast, lunch, and dinner with a small bar off the lobby and hosts corporate retreats, meetings, weddings, and other specialty events. For reservations or information: (800) 749-4466 or info@clewistoninn.com

Traveling another 16 miles north on U. S. 27 is Moore Haven, settled along the Caloosahatchee River that links the Atlantic Ocean to the Gulf of Mexico. The old town square, just beneath Highway 27 overpass, now remains silent but is reminiscent of the days when it was a thriving farm and cattle town.

For a breakfast, lunch, or dinner break in Moore Haven on U.S. 27, there is Tico's Spanish and Mexican Restaurant serving authentic, delicious dishes in pleasant surroundings with courteous service. A few blocks further west is Joey's Pizza with a menu of take out food and hot fudge sundaes, just across the street from the county seat, Moore Haven's restored courthouse.

As the highway curves another 11 miles through native habitat and pastures to Palmdale, the time clock returns 200 million years ago when ancient dinosaurs roamed the earth leaving behind today's curious reptiles: The alligators and crocodiles, both native to Florida. Palmdale is the home of the giant behemoths and one of the oldest roadside attractions, Gatorama, purchased in 1986 by "Florida Cracker" David Theilen from an alligator poacher, Cecil Clemons. Theilen's premise in buying Gatorama was that alligators would be a curious attraction to northern visitors who had never before seen the gigantic reptiles.

Today, Gatorama serves as a science center for the study of endangered crocodiles and for alligator breeding and harvesting with "hands-on" science, managed meticulously by present owners, Patty and Allen Register.

Through the gift shop, walking along the open boardwalk, crocodiles, alligators, and humans peer at each other from a safe distance as the reptiles swim underneath in surrounding ponds. The reptiles flaunt their posture with spiked tails above the water giving a sense of each creature's size. As the eye moves toward the triangular head of the crocodile, or the rounded muzzle of the alligator snout, Patty Register gives a guided tour to visitors explaining the difference between the two ancient beasts.

Gatorama began with a clutch of 800 alligators and today has expanded to more than 4,500. The largest alligator on sight, Goliath, weighs 1,000 pounds and is approximately 14 feet long. Gatorama also harvests alligators for meat and hides that they sell at the gift shop. Gatorama is open seven days a week, rain or shine, from 9 am to 6 p.m. Cost of admission: $11.95 adults and children 56 inches and shorter, $5.95; plus, you can take a picture holding an alligator.

For special groups, there is a "Gator Shining Night" to tour the park as the sun sets, and enjoy a home-cooked "cracker style" meal including alligator tail, swamp cabbage, and sour orange pie. Reservations are required. Call (863) 675-0623 or visit www.gatorama.com.

Fighting crocodiles
Photograph by Alan Register

One mile north of Gatorama, on the west side U.S. 27 is Fisheating Creek open for camping, canoeing/kayaking, swimming and peaceful walks through the woods. Fisheating Creek is 52 miles long and is filled with native catfish, brim, and bass. The park covers 28,000 acres and is also one of the largest nesting areas of the migratory Swallowtail Kite that travels from Brazil every spring to build nests in the tall trees along the Creek. There are also great white herons, egrets, and wild turkeys. Alligators, mud turtles, and bobcats roam the cypress hammocks rising along the tannic creek waters from the crystal white "sugar sand" that once was the bottom of the ocean before the last Ice Age when Florida arose from the depths.

Fisheating Creek is on the lower section of the Lake Whales Ridge that curves up the spine of Florida some 200 miles north and is a unique eco-system of paleo-islands that never sunk as Florida's sea-levels fluctuated over millions of years.

Fisheating Creek's headwater flows from Highlands County to the north and meanders through marshes, pastures, forests, winding into Lake Okeechobee. The early Indians used the creek as a trade route to Punta Gorda and early settlers used it to deliver mail.

Fisheating Creek provides 100 campsites with full hook-ups and primitive sites. The cost is $20.00 nightly for a full hook-up, monthly sites are $500.00 plus tax, and primitive sites run from $10 (off the creek) and $15.00 on the creek. The campground provides a small country store for staples, local newspapers, ice, and information on guided eco-tours. Canoe rentals are $30.00 for a full day with a day trip to Burnt Bridge, $20.00, or a two day trip to Ingram's Crossing at $25.00.

The beauty of Fisheating Creek is a place where the only night lights are a canopy of stars over the warmth of a campfire and the aroma of roasting hotdogs. Fishing, swimming, relaxing is the attraction for visitors here to forget the burdens of the city and refresh in Nature. The address: 7555 U.S. Highway 27 N, Palmdale, Florida 33944. (863) 675-5999. www. fisheatingcreekresort.com

Moving less than a mile north along U.S. 27, past Palmdale's old country store, is Vanishing Species Wildlife Preserve, open Thursday through Sunday, 9:30-4:30 p.m. Vanishing Species Wildlife is a haven to a variety of non-releasable bears, primates, big cats, reptiles, and other animals. Jeff Harrod,

Jeff Harrod and Daisy

owner, provides educational programs designed to entertain and educate all age groups about wildlife, the environment, and protecting endangered species. Vanishing Species new resident is "Daisy," a 2 month old bear rescued out of Ohio. With a broad knowledge of reptiles and mammals, Harrod fearlessly wraps himself in a giant Columbian Boa Constrictor captured in nearby LaBelle that he explains was apparently released into the wild.

Inside the attraction, visitors can stroll through a herpetarium of venomous and non-venomous reptiles and ponder ancient relics featured in the history museum. There is a gift shop and just outside, a family picnic area to feed goats, sheep, and other livestock that roam freely. Call (954) 347-1404 for admission and tours or www.VanishingSpecies.net/palmdale.

In this unspoiled corner of "old Florida," little known by many who bypass this destination, Glades County provides a rare serenity that tingles the spine and rekindles the spirit and can only be discovered in the last pristine wilderness.

LIVING IN HARMONY WITHOUT FEAR OF NATURE
BY
NANCY DALE
FOR THE GLADES DEMOCRAT
MAY 22, 2008

Palmdale, on the shoulder of Lake Okeechobee, is one of the last pristine wilderness areas in Florida surrounded by large oaks, stately cabbage palms, and gentle meandering Fisheating Creek that echoes with a cacophony of crickets into the night sky. But, amidst the serenity of this quiet environment, nature's creatures still rule, sometimes shriveling man's self-importance, when paths cross unexpectedly.

On December 1st, as the blazoned orange and lavender sky was shading into dusk, it was the close of another day as I prepared to depart from the peaceful refuge of my 1952 Spartan trailer. Reaching, as I have done thousands of times before, into the darkness of a musty cabinet near the floor, I felt a quick prick on the thumb and briskly withdrew my arm into the light. As I examined the ruffled skin on my thumb, I began to observe in less than 3 seconds, motley circles of blue and black swirling quickly around my rapidly swelling finger. Apparently, hibernating in this cozy dark spot was a small pygmy rattler that was surprised and disturbed as I reached into "its" space. Perhaps, we were both astonished, as I brushed my appendage over its cold body and instinctively, the little creature reacted out of self-preservation, just as I did when I quickly withdrew my arm from the cabinet. Just a naturally as if the little snake was hiding underneath a log and felt threatened, it issued a bite that was either "dry" (not fully releasing a full fang of venom) or a what could have been a deadly warning.

Not knowing for sure, or wanting to believe I had been bitten by a venous snake, I hesitated to react too seriously as there was no blood or severe pain. However, there was no denying, I knew from research that a finger turning black was a venous snakebite moniker. After all of these years, "fate" had called my card. It wasn't the near brushes with charging bumble bees, arched-tailed stingers of scorpions, or the visiting family of hogs, it was a snake in the trailer that made Nature's presence felt. But, this time I was lucky, I lost no finger digits and other than some lingering muscle tension in the arm after a month or so, I had no other affects. Luckily, Jeff Harrod of Vanishing Species down the road got me into an ambulance and I was at Lake Placid hospital within half an hour should I have needed anti-venom which they have.

Six months have passed, and I have pondered, researched, talked with ranchers, exterminators, and others about how to return to the trailer and slide my feet under the covers in my bed and sleep soundly without the vision of giant fangs and a wet cold body slipping underneath the sheets to nuzzle down beside me into a warm cozy space.

Finally, I got the courage to go back to the trailer with Jeff who came inside, shook all the sheets out, opened the closets and the cabinet. No sign of any creatures. Jeff recommended that I stay the night, but I couldn't quite bring myself to be that brave, yet. But I did sit inside for a long time, uncorked a bottle of wine, turned on some calming music, and picked-up where I left off. I climbed up on my sawhorse bed, opened wide the curtains and watched the blazoned sun sink into a lavender sky as the afternoon faded into dusk. On this day, I felt safe.

Snake handler at Brighton Field Days

THE NEW PIONEERS: CAPITALIZING ON THE EMERGING ECONOMIES IN GLADES/HENDRY COUNTIES

Nancy Dale, keynote address to the Inaugural Graduating Leadership Class of the Glades/ Hendry County EDCs

June 16, 2007

Culminating six months of interactive workshops and seminars, twenty graduates of the inaugural leadership class of Glades/Hendry County Economic Development Councils received their diploma June 16, 2007 at the Clewiston Country Club with more than one hundred guests in attendance. Janice Groves, Hendry EDC Executive Director and Emcee Dan Regelski, Director of the Small Business Development Center at Florida Gulf Coast University, congratulated the graduates and encouraged them to take the foreground in leadership for the community.

Kevin Thomas of CHL and EDC Board Member introduced each graduate and highlighted the accomplishments that qualified them as selected participants in the program who plan to move forward with individual goals and objectives to accomplish over the coming year.

The keynote address was presented by Glades County author, Dr. Nancy Dale, with a message to "*The New Pioneers: Capitalizing on the Emerging Economies in Glades/Hendry Counties.*"

"Moving forward into a vision of the future, often means looking back from where we started," said Dr. Dale talking about the two hundred year cultural heritage of the Florida pioneer "cow hunters" who settled Florida in the 1800s and those that came before dating back to the Paleo-Indians, and later Ponce de Leon in the 1500s who named Florida, "the land of flowers."

"With a state population today of 18 million, up more than 300,000 since last year, we are not going to stop growth; however, we do need to manage it and attract the urban dollars into Glades/Hendry Counties for more jobs, an expanded tax base, and career opportunities for our youth."

The emerging economies are based on what Dr. Dale termed a triangulation of nature-based/cultural heritage tourism; new green communities incorporating agriculture and habitat; and an educational consortium for the development of 21st century sustainable "green industry" technologies that provide career opportunities and economic spin offs for local businesses.

In the arena of renewable energy, Dr. Dale cited the examples of "Alico, Inc. in LaBelle investigating a cellulosic ethanol project using a $13 million grant from the Department of Energy, and Citrus Energy, LLC in Clewiston planning to construct a 4 million gallon per year ethanol bio-refinery using citrus waste projected to produce 80 million gallons of ethanol a year."

Dr. Dale referenced state and national research regarding the fast growing emerging multi-billion dollar economies that can be marketed and capitalized upon in Glades/Hendry Counties, emphasizing "first what we already have here in this last vast, valuable land in Florida, our nature-based and cultural heritage tourism. More than 78.6 million people visit Florida every year with an impact of $57 billion dollars on the state economy; 189 million Americans hike, trek or travel into wilderness areas, or 94.5% of the population. Regionally, nature-based and cultural heritage tourism increased nearby county coffers, such as Charlotte Harbor watershed with more than $3.2 billion a year into the area and $1.8 billion a year to Florida. Glades/Hendry Counties needs to attract dollars to our pristine wilderness and cultural heritage sites, the later which additionally draws to the region more than 200,000 people."

Dr. Dale said that Glades/Hendry Counties need to cultivate regionally a marketing image to attract more of the urban tourist dollar. She said that beaches and condos are "a dime a dozen" but that Glades/Hendry Counties "provide a unique pristine wilderness and heritage that is unique, like no other place in the world. It is a refuge from the pollution, traffic, stress and by-products of the city. People are paying to escape."

"Incubating and capitalizing on new economies means crossing the chasm into creating highly valuable and sustainable use of the areas most valuable asset: Land," said Dr. Dale. "Growth means not only marketing nature-based-cultural heritage tourism, but the triangulation of the $12 billion 'green industry' in collaboration with educational consortiums such as Florida Gulf Coast University and Edison College to develop affordable 'green' housing in collaboration with the Florida Green Builders Association " Pointing to a planned new "green" community in rural Calhoun County, "Sky Project," was recently awarded $1.8 million by Governor Crist along with Florida State University's Advanced Power Systems and consortium to pay for geothermal and solar energy applications in the 624 home sites on 571 acres in Crestview about one hour from Tallahassee. The new community will dedicate half of the development to agriculture to bring back the rural centerpiece of the farmers market providing opportunities for home owners as small farmers and the opportunity to contribute to the $14 billion organic market. Presently, there are 77 green markets in cities across Florida." Dr. Dale said that "with agriculture in Hendry/Glades County having a long-time economic presence, Hendry County's market value of crops is more than $375,000 contributing to the $87 billion agricultural industry, it is vital lifeblood in Florida. Ed Kuester of the office of the Florida Commissioner of Agriculture said that Florida's "rural land base has experienced a five-fold increase in urban conversion from 1964 to 1997. This increase in urban land use resulted in the loss of nearly 5 million acres of valuable agricultural land during this period. According to University of Florida research, we can expect to lose another 1.3 million acres of land to urban conversion over the next ten years." Dr. Dale added that with these numbers "we cannot be in a situation to depend on foreign countries for our food supply. If new communities can incorporate agriculture, we can at least save some of the land and further develop local green markets for our food source."

Dr. Dale said that in terms of dollars into rural Calhoun County from the new Sky Project community/agriculture concept, "it is expected to bring $22 million into the county tax fund within 12 years. Additionally, through university consortiums such as FSU assisting in the development of renewal geo-thermal and solar energy for Sky Project, these consortiums offer future careers in the billion dollar 21st Century "green technology" industry for the rural areas. In land use preservation, such as Sky Project, the new green community incorporates native habitat, open space and agriculture. Also in terms of dollars, there are federal tax incentives for green home builders, tenants, and by 2008 there is expected to be a federal tax deduction for the use of green energy. On Yahoo's web page, there is currently a contest for the "Greenest Community in Florida" with a cash prize of $250,000 or 10 hybrid taxis."

However, housing/accommodations are a concern to attract new industries. To create affordable housing, Dr. Dale said that the "unique pioneer heritage of Glades/Hendry County can be capitalized into dollars for second home getaways for urbanites wanting to escape the city, and affordable housing for locals with new communities supporting both low and high end green "cracker houses" and log homes that also provide 21st Century technology such as wireless internet.,

In closing, Dr. Dale paraphrased poet Robert Frost's poem, "The Road Not Taken," to the graduates as the Glades/Hendry County entrepreneurs moving forward, following a path where "it bends into the undergrowth" and cannot be seen beyond the curve but encouraged the graduates to take the "road less traveled" into the future, leading the community in preservation of the land and cultural heritage in the sustainable growth of green industry communities and technology of the 21st century. In a final note, Dr. Dale posed a question to the graduates: "What is the vision of Glades/Hendry Counties ten years from now?"

At the end of the ceremony, graduates received a gift packet with a copy of two books: A Land Remembered by Patrick Smith and a personally inscribed copy of Would Do, Could Do and Made Do: The Pioneer Cow Hunters Who Tamed the Last Frontier by Nancy Dale..

The graduates:

Clifton Baldwin, Jr. First Bank of Clewiston
Derek Beck, Beck Construction
Sherri Denning, Southern Land Real Estate
Jeni Dyess, Florida Community Bank
Neftali Francisco Fernandez, M.D., Florida Dept. of Health, Hendry/Glades County Health Dept.
Angela Hall, Port LaBelle Resorts, LLC
Estela Hernandez, Hendry County EDC
LaVita Holmes, Self-Employed – Quick Release Bail Bonds, Owner

Thomas Misotti, Owen-Ames-Kimball Company & Talkin' Monkeys Project
Sean Moore, Clewiston Chamber of Commerce
Mark Morton, Lykes Bros.
Steven Nisbet, Nisbet Enterprises – DBA McDonald's Restaurants
Cathy Perry, Home & Ranch Real Estate Company
Denise Roth, Southern Gardens Citrus
Wayne Simmons, Heritage Land Company
Kevin Thomas, CHL Holdings, Inc.
Danielle Toms, Glades Electric Cooperative
Sara Townsend, LaBelle Chamber of Commerce
Glenda Wilson, Hendry Regional Medical Center
Ronald Zimmerly, Hendry County, Grants & Special Projects.

A SHORT DRIVE TO AN OKEECHOBEE REFUGE
ARNOLD'S WILDLIFE REHABILITATION CENTER

Looking for a nearby retreat to kick-back and enjoy nature? The centerpiece at Arnold's Wildlife Rehabilitation Center in Okeechobee is a lush half-acre butterfly garden where visitors can stroll through a setting of more than 2000 native plants that provide a habitat for hundreds of butterflies. Arnold's Butterfly Haven is an extension of the wildlife conservation efforts of the Center which devotes more than ten acres to homeless and injured animals. Visitors are welcomed into an "ever-changing garden in motion," as described by Sue Arnold, owner and trained rehabilitation specialist who treats rescued animals delivered to her care by Fish and Wildlife and individuals who find injured wildlife.

The garden replaces what was previously an orange grove destroyed during Hurricanes Frances and Jeanne in 2004. Once the wreckage of stumps and overturned trees were bulldozed away, Arnold felt the best use of the land was as a haven for butterflies which suffer from diminishing habitat due to human encroachment.

"The butterfly garden grew out of my own search for peace when my daughter passed on a few years ago. I wanted to create a place of serenity not only for me, but for others who visit the Rehabilitation Center. It became part of my own rehabilitation," says Arnold. "The garden of more than sixty species of free-roaming butterflies includes the habitat of the rarely seen green and black Malachite and the Cuban Crescent." But, the life of these small delightful creatures grace nature for only a short time. "Beginning its first stage as a caterpillar that hatches from an egg laid by a female, it, devours the host plant, forms a chrysalis, and through metamorphosis becomes a beautiful butterfly. The process takes only a few weeks, but they live only about two weeks then the cycle begins again," adds Arnold.

Hundreds of butterflies are attracted to the garden's abundant larval (host) and flowering nectar plants where they stop to unfurl their proboscis (feeding tube) to suck-up the sweet nectar. "The Butterfly Haven reflects a balanced eco-system for the cold blooded beauties that gravitate to heat to lay their eggs, especially during summer. Arnold says that "on the hottest day of the year, you can be sitting in the garden with hundreds of butterflies clustering around and on you." Many of the garden's flowering plants are donated by butterfly clubs around the state as the Center operates strictly on private donations. "We do not buy any of our butterflies. With the plight of increased urbanization, we provide not only a refuge for butterflies and animals but a place where Mother Nature maintains a balanced setting of bugs, wasps, and birds in this circle of life," Arnold emphasizes. The garden, shaped like Florida's state butterfly the Zebra Longwing, has "a motion that blends into the natural, open setting," Arnold describes.

Arnold's Wildlife Rehabilitation Center and Butterfly Haven not only attracts native species but more than ten thousand people a year who stroll along the maze of walkways to view up-close and personal, many animals on the premises. There are the Florida panthers (pumas) Arnold raised as babies; the bobcats; Ringtail lemurs, aptly named "Maddie" and "Gascar," classified as an endangered species from Madagascar; South American prehensile tailed porcupines; Kinkajous from South America;; free-roaming peacocks, chickens, egrets, and visiting sandhill cranes. There is Professor Opossum, popular with children that travels with Arnold to local schools giving students the opportunity to observe and feel the furry animal, introducing him with an educational lecture. Arnold also offers guided tours at the Center for visiting school groups, speaks to many local organizations, and at fundraisers.

Sue Arnold has treated thousands of animals, nursed them back to health through bottle feedings with tender loving care, set broken wings and legs, mended injuries from automobile accidents, and helped wildlife recover from desertion or neglect. She trained under a licensed rehabilitation specialist and has a degree in medical technology. She opened the center some 12 years ago and is assisted totally by volunteers. Eleven year old, Maggie Bucina and Sue's intern Angela Waldron, prepare prescribed food for each animal. Local veterinarians Drs. Jim Letcher and Jim Harvey of Okeechobee provide emergency services and visits as well as Dr. Lee Corbridge of Sebring. The Center is licensed by Florida Fish and Wildlife and the USDA. The Center, open 7 days a week, lends an opportunity for visitors to watch a release of some of the rehabilitated animals back into the wild, such as the six Bard Owls that recently reclaimed their natural territory lifting into the wind on wings of freedom.

Arnold's Wildlife Rehabilitation Center and Butterfly Haven is located at 14895 N. 30th Terrace, Okeechobee, Florida. Hours: 7 days 10-4 p.m. Adult admission: $10.00 and children 12 and under free. Specially priced admission is charged for school or other large groups but need to call ahead for a tour schedule. Contact Arnold's Wildlife at 863-763-4630 or visit the website www.arnoldswildlife.org for directions.

A TWO HOUR TIME WARP INTO FLORIDA'S PRE-HISTORY

HIGHLANDS HAMMOCK STATE PARK

The "12 Hours of Sebring" in Central Florida is the famous Formula One Grand Prix race where every March world class drivers thrill thousands of fans challenging their agility and endurance. However, high-speed racing is not the only attraction in Sebring, it is also a place to slow down and travel back into Florida's pre-history, the Age of Coal and Conifers (Pennsylvanian Period that began 250 million years ago) in the ancient Cypress Swamp of giant ferns and hardwood forests of "real Old Florida" at Highlands Hammock State Park. It is a short day trip from Florida's east coast but a journey millions of years back in time.

The story of Florida's natural history at the park remains unspoiled for motorists, bicycle riders, in-line skaters that travel along the 3.2 mile paved loop road beneath an arching canopy. The cry of Red-Shouldered Hawks and Pileated Woodpeckers echoes through the tall Cypress and some 1,000 year old Oaks as they weave beneath their protective shield. The ancient hammock (defined as higher ground than its surroundings) is characterized by hardwood vegetation and deep, humus-rich soil where visitors can hike nine wooded trails, or stroll along several elevated boardwalks. The most popular thirty minute hike is the Cypress Swamp Trail and "catwalk" built across Charlie Bowlegs Creek where photographers can shoot close-up pictures of alligators swimming below as Wood Storks and White Ibis wade through tannic waters immersed only in the natural sound of wildlife.

Only six miles west of Sebring, away from the fast pace of urban life, Highlands Hammock is one of the first four state parks established in Florida. "The idea of establishing a park at what locals called 'Hooker's Hammock' was a goal of several businessmen in the 1930s. They shared their plans with Mrs. Margaret Shippen Roebling who along with her family donated funds to purchase land for the park and began construction," explains Park Services Specialist Dorothy Harris. Raymond Greene also an early supporter managed the nearby $30 million dollar Spanish Style Harder Hall Hotel overlooking Little Lake Jackson. The famous "1900s Boom Day" Harder Hall Hotel had a brief heyday then closed when the developer died in a plane crash. Today, its future still hangs in the balance as the hotel is closed but its beautiful pink towers still loom over the Lake attracting the attention of curious travelers on U.S. 27.

At the park you can hike or choose to ride the tram on a ranger-guided tour and enjoy their extensive knowledge about bobcats, panthers, river otters, flora and fauna of the Park's unique native habitat. If you are a horseback rider, there is an equestrian trail for your pleasure (a negative Coggins Test must be presented prior to using the trail). When you're hungry, there are delicious dishes served-up fresh at the Highlands Hammock Inn, a historic structure built by the Civilian Conservation Corp (CCC) in the early 1930s.

The story of the CCC is told in the Museum (across from the Highlands Hammock Inn). It was after the 1929 stock market crash when an adjoining section of land was purchased for the CCC that provided needed jobs and for the groundbreaking of the Florida Botanical Garden and Arboretum to be located in the park. During WWII the project was abandoned and the garden never completed. Today, Highlands Hammock State Park has expanded to over 9,000 acres of preserved land," adds Harris with camping and other recreational activities/facilities.

Just off loop road is a large open Amphitheatre framed by the woods in an ample clearing with rows of wooden benches for rustic seating. This is a site of frequent weddings and celebrations. There is also an on-site Recreation Hall available for rent. Call 863-386-6094 to reserve these facilities or the open air picnic pavilion.

Just beyond the park's entrance is a spacious campground nestled beneath tall shady oaks. The year round camping fee is $18.00 plus tax with a Florida resident senior citizen or disabled discount available. For reservations visit: www.ReserveAmerica.com or call 1-800-326-3521. Pets are welcome in all outdoor areas in the park but must be confined on a six foot leash. The daily admission fee is $4.00 per vehicle, up to eight people, or $3.00 for a single occupant. Highlands Hammock State Park is open 365 days a year.

Driving directions to the park from the east coast: Take Highway 70 west through Okeechobee to U.S. Highway 27. Travel north on U.S, 27 to Sebring and turn west on County Road 634 (Hammock Road), the park entrance is four miles.

Highlands Hammock State Park is a place of respite, relaxation, recreation, and where to experience the natural beauty of old Real Florida.

FOLKLIFE: RANCHING TRADITIONS THE FLORIDA FOLK FESTIVAL

STEPHEN FOSTER STATE PARK – WHITE SPRINGS

On a breezy Memorial Day Weekend 2008, thousands of people, many who have attended the Florida Folk festival for more than 30 years, were entertained by a showcase of Florida cattle ranchers featured in the "Folklife Area" of Florida Cattle Ranching Traditions.

Everything from whip cracking, storytelling, cooking and occupational arts were displayed and demonstrated by men and women who have practiced their trade as a way of life since Florida was settled by early "cow hunters" and "huntresses" more than 200 years ago.

The public had the opportunity to pet and feed hay to Mark Carpenter's (Levy County) cracker cattle and roan cracker horse trained by Amanda, one of his four children. Little tykes with hands full of hay were greeted by three young calves who graciously accepted their offerings to the thrill of some who may have only seen a cow in the movies or a magazine.

The amazing talent of "metallurgy" and sculpturing, more simply described as the artistic craft of custom building spurs, bits, branding irons, door knockers, stirrups and silhouettes (above entrance gateways) is the talent of Billy Davis (Kenansville). Patiently explaining a craft that has a language of its own, Billy Davis and his wife Cynthia display a representation of history with gear worn or used by "cow hunters," cattlemen and women as trademarks of the industry.

Cooking up her specialties and talking about the cattlewomen's contributions to Florida's heritage is Imogene Yarborough (Seminole County). Honored with recognition in the Florida Agriculture Hall of Fame, Imogene Yarborough says that "whether it is 1 acre or 1,000, we call a 'ranch' our home. It means that we have all kinds of animals and agriculture, so important in all of our lives." However, Imogene says that often when she talks to "politicians" the "first word out of their mouth is, 'I am a rancher.' This may not always hold true but they want you to believe they are one of you." Incorporating the story of how the Florida cattle industry rose to one of the State's most important components of the agriculture industry and ranking among the top producers in the United States, Imogene herself part of the cultural heritage, continues to promote Florida beef. "Cattle women started going into the grocery stores demonstrating how to properly cook beef, not just throwing it on a grill. Then, we educated the children as we asked them questions about where they get their meat or milk. Many said they get it at Publix. So we developed an educational program." Since the passing of her husband, Edmund, Imogene says that many widowed cattle women continue to run the ranch, just as she does in Geneva near the St. John's River.

Also featured in interviews and discussions were Willie Johns (Brighton Seminole Historian), Paul Bowers (Big Cypress Reservation), Mack Padget (Lake Wales), Tom Everett (Sumter County), Jose Carlos Martinez (Dade County), and Eldon Lux (Kenansville). Talking up a storm with their verbal  cowboy poetry were Hank Matson (Lake Placid), Carl Sharp (LaBelle), Butch Harrison (Delray), and Doyle Rigdon (Okeechobee). The crowd circled around the story tellers stage just as if was a campfire with embers floating into an ink jet sky surrounded in a silence descending like dew upon avid listeners interrupted only by laughter and applause.

 Echoing from the Folklife stage, meandering through the tall cabbage palms, pines and oaks was a variety of music strummed, sung, fiddled, beat, and bellowed by Wayne Martin (Blountstown) and champion fiddler; Emilio Ortiz of Colombian heritage, who squeezed the accordion with traditional folk music of the region.

Buddy Mills (Okeechobee), who learned to make buckskin whips from his father, "Junior" Wills was on hand to explain how he builds the famous cracker whips used as signals for cow crews on cattle drives and gathering cattle. His son Chad and Buddy's wife, Jessica who work on their Okeechobee ranch, revealed their traditional recipe for making swamp cabbage, handed-down by Buddy's daddy.

DELICATE TRADITIONS

Today's cowmen and women go about the everyday chores of gathering and parting cattle, carrying on traditional practices handed down as the "cow hunter" ways over generations, as well as incorporating 21st Century technology in raising, breeding and selling cattle through the internet and traditional livestock markets. However, cattlemen and women have always employed the best methodologies of preserving and utilizing all parts of the cattle from hooves to hides. Besides sophisticated DNA testing used to determine beef marbling for cattle going to the breadbasket of America and other counties, part of the process includes "cutting" (castrating) selected male calves to become steers.

For the urban raised individual, a special delicacy, well-known over the years to "cow hunters" and cowmen/women are the "rocky mountain oysters." Jessica Mills, rancher, barrel racer and wife of Buddy Mills expert "cracker whip" builder calls "rocky mountain oysters," or tender veal testicles as "scrumptious," especially the way she cooks them up. "To prepare this appetizer delicacy, you dust the testicles with flour, salt and pepper then fry them to a golden brown. That's all you have to do, but other spices or flavoring can also be added. We have them whenever there is a two to four month old bull calf in our herd that has been cut." Not only does Jessica prepare the "rocky mountain oysters" appetizer, she also works together with her son, Chad and Buddy performing the castrations. "Several young calves can be cut in just a few minutes," says Buddy Mills.

Billy Davis, Buddy Miles, and Mark Carpenter cutting a bull

"You cut as many bull calves as a rancher wants. You hold one leg and sit on another one while the calf is down on its side. With a sharp knife you cut the scrota, reach in and pull out the testicles that are cut from the vasdeferens which recede inside. You pull the testicles out first and the rest you leave intact. There is some bleeding but the wound heals by itself," explains Buddy Mills.

Others who displayed their craft at the Folklife festival was Ned Waters (Bartow) who makes nylon whips; Trevor Manley, Mack Padgett's grandson dazzled the crowd with his whip popping talent as well as Poppy Moe (Ocala), a lady team roper and horse trainer. Moe also crafts custom-made chaps, chinks (short chaps), and leather works for working cowboys and rodeo competitors.

The Seminole tribe, who are traditional Florida cattle ranchers, greeted visitors at the Ee-to-lit-kee, Seminole Family Camp and giant Chickee (house). Working at a table, Jennie Shore demonstrated how to make native coiled and twilled basketry from sweetgrass that today are made from palmettos. The baskets are used by Seminoles in which to make corn meal. Other Seminole artisans, Nancy Shore, Josephine Villa, and Addie Osceola were on hand to explain the intricate craftsmanship in designing and sewing colorful Seminole jackets, as well as beads, and palmetto fiber made dolls. In the art of wood-crafting were alligators, birds and spoons made by Victor Billie. Stirring up samples of fry bred, a traditional food of Seminoles along with sofkee (a corn, hominy meal drink) and explaining how game meats are cooked was Lorene Gopher and Molly Jolly. The public also learned about other traditional foods in the Seminole diet.

Telling a history through stories, Seminole historian Willie Johns added humor and dismay discussing the role of early settlers and U.S. government's effort to what he says was to exterminate the Seminoles as a result of the Seminole Removal Act of 1891 preventing further unification of the tribe that eventfully emerged with their own government as the Seminole Tribe of Florida in 1957. Willie Johns says "I have been in cattle all my life. My mom raised cattle and that is all I wanted to do. My bother Josiah Johns has been a long time rodeo participant. The Seminoles organized around the rodeo as they were broke and it was a way to make money besides agriculture which is a mainstay of the tribe. Today, our goal is to supply more than 1 million pounds of beef to the Hard Rock cafés owned by the Tribe."

The Florida folklore of the "cow hunter" and "cow huntress" is legendary and remains a living history over thousands of acres of land weaved through the last remaining prairies, scrub, and swampland of old and new urbanized Florida. The Florida Folk Festival paid homage to this traditional heritage and way of life that gave birth to the Florida cattle industry. *(Nancy Dale is author of Where the Swallowtail Kite Soars: The Legacies of Glades County, Florida and the Vanishing Wilderness. For other books: www. nancydalephd.com)*

THOUGHTS TO LIVE BY....

WORK LIKE YOU DON'T NEED TO WORK...
LOVE LIKE YOU'VE NEVER LOST...
DANCE LIKE NOBOBY'S WATCHING

Printed in the United States
132864LV00003B/142-198/P